Free Your Inner Nonfiction Writer

Educate, Influence, and Entertain Your Readers

Johanna Rothman

Free Your Inner Nonfiction Writer

Educate, Influence, and Entertain Your Readers

Johanna Rothman

ISBN 978-1-943487-25-7

Practical **ink**

No part of this book may be reproduced or transmitted in any form or by any means, electronic or mechanical, including photocopying, recording or by any information storage and retrieval system, without written permission from the author.

Every precaution was taken in the preparation of this book. However, the author and publisher assumes no responsibility for errors or omissions, or for damages that may result from the use of information contained in this book.

Many of the designations used by manufacturers and sellers to distinguish their products are claimed as trademarks. Where those designations appear in this book, and Practical Ink was aware of a trademark claim, the designations have been printed in initial capital letters or in all capitals.

© 2022 Johanna Rothman

In honor and memory of Jerry Weinberg. Thank you for helping me learn to write.

And, for Mark, as always.

Contents

Acknowledgments i

Introduction iii

1. **Write to Think and Learn** 1
   - 1.1 Writing Captures Words 2
   - 1.2 Reset Your Writing Rules 3
   - 1.3 Nonfiction Writers Write at Several Levels 4
   - 1.4 Fear Paralyzes Writers 5
   - 1.5 Manage Your Imposter Syndrome 10
   - 1.6 Try Freewriting 10
   - 1.7 Evolve Your Writing System 13
   - 1.8 Practice Writing to Think and Learn 13

2. **Write Fast to Write Well** 15
   - 2.1 Create Your Idea Bank and Fieldstones 15
   - 2.2 Write What Interests You 19
   - 2.3 Finish What You Start 20
   - 2.4 Cycle for Clarity 23
   - 2.5 See How to Write Fast and Well 24
   - 2.6 Write Clean to Maintain Momentum 31
   - 2.7 Practice Correct Spelling 33
   - 2.8 Practice Writing Faster to Write Well 34

3. **Write for Your Ideal Reader** 35
   - 3.1 Empathize with Your Readers 35

CONTENTS

	3.2	Write About What Matters	36
	3.3	Organize with the Rule of Three	40
	3.4	Hook The Reader with a Problem	42
	3.5	Structure Your Piece with Logic	45
	3.6	End With a Reminder of the Start	51
	3.7	Write In Any Order	51
	3.8	Practice Writing for Your Ideal Reader	52
4.	**Edit Just Enough**		55
	4.1	Edit When You're Still Interested	55
	4.2	Maintain Your Author Voice	57
	4.3	Edit as Little as Possible	58
	4.4	Review Your Logic	66
	4.5	Maintain Your Author Voice	68
	4.6	Add References	69
	4.7	Finalize Your Title	70
	4.8	Practice Editing Just Enough	72
5.	**Choose the Feedback You Want**		75
	5.1	What Will Feedback Offer You?	75
	5.2	Never Ask for Interim Feedback	76
	5.3	When Feedback Makes Sense	77
	5.4	Clarify the Value of Peer Review	78
	5.5	Consider the Perfection Game	79
	5.6	Use These Questions for Feedback	80
	5.7	Offer Feedback with Empathy	81
	5.8	Beware of Reviewer-Focused Feedback	82
	5.9	Build Your Peer Community	83
	5.10	Create a Writing Community	84
	5.11	Practice Your Feedback Choices	84
6.	**Publish Your Work**		85
	6.1	You Own Your Writing	85
	6.2	Your Employer Owns Your Writing	86
	6.3	Write as Work for Hire	87

6.4	Write for Publishers Who Don't Want Your Copyright	89
6.5	How to Work with a Professional Editor	89
6.6	Choose Your Publication Options	90
6.7	Recognize When Others Violate Your Copyright	93
6.8	Publish Widely	94
6.9	Practice Publishing Your Work	95

7. Help Yourself Succeed 97

7.1	Create Your Writing Environment	97
7.2	Count Your Words	99
7.3	Avoid Talking About Your Writing	100
7.4	Read Widely	101
7.5	Write With Others	103
7.6	Transform Your Perfection Rules	104
7.7	Watch for These Writing Traps	105
7.8	Last Words—For Now	108

Annotated Bibliography 109

More from Johanna 111

Acknowledgments

I thank all the writers who've taken my writing workshops. I have learned much from you. I also thank Rebecca Airmet for her editing.

Cover image: Depositphotos 3319755, author: alphaspirit

Cover by Brandon Swann, swanndesignstudio.com

Introduction

You'd like to write better or faster, but everything you do seems to slow you down. Or, maybe you start to write but you don't finish what you started. Even if you finish, your writing doesn't resonate with the very people it should.

Maybe you take "too long" to write. Or you have the face-the-blank-page problem, the am-I-good-enough problem, and other worries.

You might think of these challenges as "writing" problems. They're not. They're system problems—and when you write, you expose your systemic problems.

If you can create a successful system for your writing, you can eliminate those problems and write well. You can choose how to create systems that work for you.

That's how you free your inner writer. Learn what does work for you. You can learn to write fast and well, and to offer value to your ideal readers.

You can write nonfiction that educates, influences, and entertains.

Maybe you think I'm a "natural" writer. Not at all. I was not born with a pen in my hand. I've learned to write through practice and experimentation. I'm sharing what I've learned with you in this book.

Early in my management career, I asked a colleague for feedback on a memo I wrote. The feedback: "A verb, JR, you need a verb somewhere in these thirty words." I've learned to write shorter sentences, each with a verb. Sometimes, two verbs.

Since then, I've published twenty books, thousands of blog posts, and hundreds of articles. Then there's all the emails, conference proposals, and reports for my clients.

If you write these kinds of nonfiction, this book is for you:

- Expository nonfiction, such as a memo or a report
- Personal essay
- Articles, blog posts, or other short writing that explains or informs readers.

Writers write nonfiction because they need to share the how, why, or what for a reader who wants to learn more.

If you write other kinds of nonfiction, you might benefit from the ideas here, but no guarantees. I focused this book on the short forms of nonfiction. These ideas also work for book chapters, but might not be sufficient for you to write a book.

Given that, let's start with how you can create your writing practice to free your inner writer.

1. Write to Think and Learn

Nonfiction writers encounter several problems:

- The blank page staring back at you, taunting you.
- Not knowing what to write about.
- Wondering how to structure this piece so people read it.

You might even have more concerns.

You've been writing for years—maybe even since you were seven or eight years old. Why is writing so hard for you?

Because no one told you this secret: When you write nonfiction, you also think and learn. As you write, you integrate what you think and learn to write more in this piece.

For most of us nonfiction writers, writing is non-linear. We write a little, realize we learned something, and write more based on what we learned. Sometimes, we cycle back to the start, and sometimes we write the end. However, as we write we integrate what we think and learn by the act of writing.

That's because when we write nonfiction, we work at several levels: how to explain the problem(s) first to ourselves, identifying the solution(s), and how to write all of that down so a reader can understand.

That means most of us need to iterate on our writing. If we think and write at the "same" time, what is writing?

1.1 Writing Captures Words

Writing occurs when you move your pen across the page, or your fingers across the keyboard. If you dictate, you move your mouth so a recorder can "hear" you and transcribe that writing later.

Writing requires action.

Here's what writing is not:

- Making or drinking the beverage of your choice, while looking out the window.
- Thinking without moving your hands. I can compose words all I want in my head. That's not writing.
- Research. You might need to research to better understand your topic and how to frame your topic to your ideal reader. But research is not writing.

Outlining and mind mapping might help you prepare to write, to organize your thoughts. However, very few people generate words as they outline or mind map.

Writing means you create new words. That's it. Any other activity might help you prepare to write, but it's not writing.

 Writing creates words you can see.

But, you say, you need an outline because you can't write in a linear way. Over your career, you've learned that you need to go back and "fix" your words.

That's totally normal.

Nonfiction writers write from their expertise. That means we integrate thinking and learning *as we write*. That thinking and learning requires that we iterate—cycle back—and fix our ideas, to clarify what we now realize we know.

Cycling is a normal part of writing and helps you create new words.

Your English teachers—well-meaning as they were—thought you could not create new words without all that preparation. And they often thought that your preparation meant you didn't need to cycle to integrate your new thinking and learning.

There's a lot more your teachers never told you about writing. It's time to reset your writing rules.

1.2 Reset Your Writing Rules

Long ago, your English teachers taught you rules for writing, based on synthesizing information you learned. They thought those rules made it easier for them to read your writing. As long as you synthesized information, those rules worked pretty well.

However, now, you're not *only* synthesizing information. You also analyze, apply, and create new content as you write. That's how you share your expertise in your writing.

Those old writing rules based on synthesis no longer apply to you. You can reset those rules.

Here are some of those rules you can reset:

1. Edit as you write. This is the worst possible advice when you try to share your expertise. That's because as you write, you identify and explore the issues and solutions.
2. Outline before you start writing. Some writers can do this. However, if we're examining the problem and possible solutions, how can we know what those problems and solutions are until we start to write?

3. Start with a blank page. You're supposed to start with nothing and build up from there. Nothing intermediate that builds up your thinking and writing by bits.

These rules don't work for most experts who want to write effective nonfiction. That's why I say we write at several levels at once.

1.3 Nonfiction Writers Write at Several Levels

When I was in university, I studied Computer Science. I was not a "natural" programmer, any more than I am a "natural" writer. But I learned a ton about writing from my experience as a programmer:

- The computer didn't care what I meant. It only "cared" about the code I wrote. I had to use the "right" code, the right words, so the computer would do what I wanted it to do.
- My programs were only valuable to some kinds of users. Not everyone, but specific users.
- I never got the program right the first time. Never. And the larger the problem I needed to solve, the more I had to iterate on the design and the code. That's because I couldn't just *think* through the problem. I had to write a little code to expose the real issues. Then, as I learned about the real problems, I cycled through the features to finish the program.

As a programmer, I spent time identifying the problems, iterating on how to solve those problems, and then clarifying my ideas. I wrote a little code. As I checked it, I realized I missed something. I often changed some of my previously-written code, *and* added more code, not necessarily in the same file. I checked the small bits of code as I proceeded—but I rarely verified the entire program until I was all done.

Your teachers might have told you to separate your thinking and writing, especially with an outline. That approach might work when you synthesize other people's ideas.

However, the more complex the problem, the more writing looks like my programming experience. When I write, I learn what I think by writing the words. The words I already wrote help me iterate on the ideas, refining what I think and checking that my logic flows correctly. I write-to-think *and* think-to-write.

As I write, I realize what I know and what I still need to learn. That thinking and learning informs my next choice of what to write. I can't separate my thinking from my writing—and why I recommend you integrate your thinking and writing.

That's why I wait to edit until I'm all done thinking—for this piece. If I interrupt my thinking with editing, I stop thinking and learning. Too often, I stop myself from writing more words in this piece.

And that's why the simple rules you learned in school don't work for nonfiction writers who want to share their expertise. Sharing our expertise is not simple—it's a complex activity.

It's time to change how you write.

But first, let's discuss fear and why you can rethink how you feel about your writing.

1.4 Fear Paralyzes Writers

Nonfiction writers have all kinds of fears. They often name these fears as "writer's block." Here are some common what-if fears:

- Someone else wrote what I want to write?
- My writing isn't very good?
- People will judge me when they read my writing?
- I'm wrong?

- I haven't read all the research?

You might have other fears, but let's start with these.

1.4.1 Someone Else Wrote This Already

I wish I could tell you that you are writing something unique. No. Someone else has already written what you plan to write.

However, I encourage you to write anyway. Why? Those writers don't have *your* experience and expertise. If you write from your experience, you will finish a piece with a different angle than everyone else. Don't worry about someone else's writing. Worry about your own ability to explain your expertise.

In addition, it's possible your ideal readers have not read what you have. You can convey that information in a way that addresses your readers' concerns.

When people tell me they have writer's block, they often write me a long email about the fact that they can't write.

Notice, they wrote that email.

Our fears exist and they can hold us back from what we want to accomplish. However, if you're like most people, you can still capture words somehow. That's writing.

> ## Writer's Block is a Different Name for Fear
>
> Let's talk about "Writer's Block" for a minute. Do other activities block you? For example, do you ever have Walking, Speaking, or Eating block? (I'm not talking about people with psychological or other disorders. I mean us relatively normal people.)
>
> I choose when to walk, speak, and eat. Just as I choose when

> to write and what to write about. If you realize this piece of writing scares you, consider going "meta" and writing about what scares you.
>
> Recognize when fear blocks you. You have options, including changing which piece you choose to write now. But you don't have writer's block.

Recognize when you experience fear. Acknowledge that fear so you don't allow that fear to paralyze you into not writing.

If you write from your expertise and experience, you can control your fear that someone else wrote what you want to write. When you use your expertise and experience, you make that topic your own.

What about wondering if your writing is any good?

1.4.2 Is Your Writing Is Good Enough?

What does "good" writing mean to you? If I can understand a piece of writing, that might be good enough. I'll suggest more ways to make your writing understandable in Chapter 4.

But, writers are terrible judges of our writing. Especially just after we finish a chunk of writing. When Mark Kilby and I wrote *From Chaos to Successful Distributed Agile Teams*, we met every day and wrote for an hour. Some days the words flowed. We could barely keep up with our ideas and how we understood them. We felt great.

Then, there were other days. We said to each other, "The writer might not have shown up today." However, when we reviewed those words the next day, we could not tell the difference from the days where the words flowed.

You might not be satisfied with your writing—yet. That's fine. Use the ideas in this book to become a better writer. And remember, the more you practice, the better your writing will be. If you reset your writing rules, especially about editing, you will learn what makes you a better writer.

The next fear is what people will think of you.

1.4.3 You Care What Other People Think

When you write, people will have opinions of you and your writing.

However, you can't control what other people think of your writing or you. You can only make your writing as good as it can be. People will judge you by your writing. They will also judge you by your haircut, how you speak, where you live, and much more.

People have judged me for what I didn't write. (They thought I wrote exactly the opposite of what I did write.) They've judged me for what I did write. (You're a woman, how can you write that?)

Instead of worrying about what people will say, consider how to share your expertise in ways that invite people to your writing. I'll discuss this more in Chapter 3.

The well-known physicist, Richard Feynman wrote a book called, *"What Do You Care What Other People Think?"*. If you write something people don't agree with, they might stop reading what you write. Or, they might read more of what you write and offer you comments.

Understand what you know, write as well as you can, and publish. Don't allow other people to prevent you from writing.

The next fear is about being wrong.

1.4.4 You Might Be Wrong

You might worry about being wrong. That's a good thing to worry about. You can manage that fear by reading—and writing—a lot about your topics. And by asking for feedback and checking references. And if you get it wrong, you might be able to change the piece even once you publish it.

For years, I wrote a monthly column for the now-defunct *Software Development Magazine*. I wrote one column about project buffers. I wrote it down wrong in my column. I didn't realize I was wrong until I read the print version of the magazine.

Oops.

I wrote to the editor, explained what I'd done, and attached the updated, corrected version. I also asked her to post the updates with a small apology. I felt stupid. However, I didn't die. I still wrote the next month's column.

I did not let fear change my writing—except to check my facts better.

Sometimes, you fear you can't write yet because you haven't read all the research.

1.4.5 You Haven't Read All the Research

Let's assume you have specific expertise. Take a minute and write a list of what you read daily, weekly, monthly, and yearly to build and maintain that expertise.

Is it possible someone else wrote something in your area of expertise and you don't know about it yet? Absolutely.

Should you wait to write your piece because you haven't read theirs? No, absolutely not.

You might have heard of "analysis paralysis." That's the equivalent of trying to research "everything" in your field.

You can't possibly read everything, *and* do your job, *and* write to educate, influence, and entertain. Choose wisely and write.

Now that we've addressed the issues of fear, let's discuss the confidence you might need to start and maintain your writing practice. That includes managing your Imposter Syndrome.

1.5 Manage Your Imposter Syndrome

Imposter Syndrome occurs when you feel as if you are not competent. You might even feel as if you had nothing to do with your previous successes. When you write, since you're exploring the problems and possible solutions, you can "use" your Imposter Syndrome as you write. Set the context for when your ideas do work, and be explicit about when your ideas might not work. Yes, I recommend you include examples where what you suggest might not work.

For example, if I've only worked with medium-size companies on a specific problem, I can say near the end of the piece: "I have not yet tried this in small startups or Fortune 50 companies. If you do, let me know what happens."

I've used this approach in blog posts and in articles for other people's sites. When you explain where your suggestions might not work, you invite a conversation with your readers.

So if you want to write, it's time to start writing. I use freewriting as a way to start.

1.6 Try Freewriting

When we freewrite, we generate as many words as possible about one specific topic. We do *not* edit as we write. You might have learned about freewriting in school.

What do you write about? I use any of these ideas to start:

- A prompt, such as a situation that you love—or hate—to see.
- Some topic you want to know more about.
- Some specific idea you want other people to know.

What if you have very large ideas and you don't think you can make those ideas specific? Take a minute (literally, 60 seconds) and brainstorm a list of all the pieces that contribute to that large chunk of information. If a list isn't how you think, consider a mind map. Don't make it pretty.

I recommend you write on paper, so you don't edit yourself by organizing as you write. If you must write an outline, toss the ideas out in outline form, and don't worry if they are in the "correct" order. Remember, this is an idea-generation activity.

Avoid ordering this list. Instead, write them down as they occur to you.

(No, this isn't "writing" yet. It's your idea bank, and part of how I prepare to write. This might work for you, too. See Chapter 2 for more information about an idea bank.)

Now, choose one item on that list. Any item that you want. But, this is key: choose *one* idea.

Set a timer for anywhere from five to fifteen minutes. That's your timebox. Write about that one small piece for that time with one caveat: always write forward.

If you write on a computer, keep your hands typing. If you write longhand, keep your pen moving across the paper. If you dictate, continue speaking. Keep writing forward. Do not correct anything. Continue to write forward, for your timebox. If you write with a pen, feel free to use arrows to tell yourself where this sentence or paragraph might go. Continue to write forward.

But, you say, the blank page intimidates you. In that case, try any of these alternatives:

- Start with "blah, blah, blah." Yes, write the blahs until you're so bored that you start to write other words.
- Start with "Johanna is a bad person. She's making me write and I hate her. I hate her so much. I hate her because…" Then

continue. I don't mind if you hate me for several lines or several paragraphs. I suspect you'll get bored of hating me and then start to write about why you hate me.
- Go "meta" and write about why you feel nervous about writing about this topic.

Try this now. Once your timer goes off, please return to this book. I'll wait until you're done.

Now, take a look at what you wrote. That's freewriting. This is the basic building block for how to free your inner writer.

If you resisted editing, your piece might sound a lot like the way you speak. You have started to discover your writing voice.

Are your words polished? Probably not. Are your ideas logical? If you're like me, no. However, you now have valuable words on the page.

When I freewrite, I learn from the act of writing down. I don't try to get it all "right" at the start. I write something so I can learn from it. I clarify what I think as I write. And, I always learn something from the act of writing. I can take all those words and ideas and write the next part of this piece.

I hope you also learned and clarified your thinking as you freewrote. When you freewrite, you allow yourself to analyze problems and identify novel solutions.

Your teachers taught your seven-year-old self to start with an outline, because your seven-year-old self did not have the ability to learn from your writing. Instead, you organized or synthesized other people's information. You also probably didn't know how to identify problems and solutions. (I certainly didn't.)

1.7 Evolve Your Writing System

That's my writing "system:" work in 15-minute timeboxes, wait to edit until you're all done writing, and maintain your idea bank and fieldstones. Those three ideas will help you avoid "Writer's Block" and finish a given piece.

You might discover that ten- or twenty-minute blocks of time work better for you. Or that you need to write at the same time every day—or you need a different time every day.

The more you experiment with your writing system, like when to write, how long to write for, how you capture and store your ideas, and what environment makes you the most productive, the more you can decide how to evolve your writing system. I'll discuss your writing environment some more in Chapter 7.

That evolution includes how you start a piece. Even though I urged you to avoid outlining first so you can think and learn, maybe you find an outline or a mind map useful to bound your piece.

That's okay. You get to choose everything about your writing system. You can't tell what works for you until you practice. As you write, you'll create new habits. So practice how you capture words.

1.8 Practice Writing to Think and Learn

All writers get better with practice. When we practice, we reinforce the behaviors we choose to use. The more you shorten the feedback loops from starting to write until you publish, the faster you will learn.

That's why I hope you choose to practice in short timeboxes, such as fifteen minutes. You'll learn how to cycle and avoid editing. You'll learn faster how to think and learn as you write.

Consider these options for your writing practice:

1. Practice more freewriting. If you did a five-minute session before, see if you can increase the time to ten or fifteen minutes.
2. Where do you want to experiment with your writing system?
3. Do you have fears about writing I didn't address? Write them down. Ask yourself these questions:
   - What's the worst thing that could happen if this fear comes true?
   - What's the best thing that might happen?
   - How can I live with both of these answers?

Now that you've started to practice integrating thinking and learning into your writing, it's time to shatter another "rule," that you have to write slowly to write well.

2. Write Fast to Write Well

Your teachers probably told you to go slowly and plan extensively before you wrote anything. And they told you to interrupt yourself with editing.

When you do plan extensively and write slowly, your readers don't see your passion and excitement in your writing. When we show our excitement for the topic, the "right" readers will find us and respond to our writing. The passion helps us educate, influence, and entertain our readers.

If you tried freewriting in the previous chapter, you realized that you don't need an extensive plan first. You might even have cycled as you practiced your freewriting, integrating your writing with your thinking and learning.

When you write fast, you write more words. The more you write and finish—with a focus on writing well—the faster you will learn and improve.

Instead of extensive planning, consider the least amount of planning you can do. I use an idea bank and fieldstones to plan just enough to start.

2.1 Create Your Idea Bank and Fieldstones

I faced the blank page problem and struggled with my writing until I read Weinberg's *Weinberg on Writing* WOW14. That's when I learned the value of fieldstones—a word, phrase, or even a paragraph or two that captures one of my ideas—so I never started with a blank page.

For example, here are some of my fieldstones that turned into blog posts about writing (remember, these are *my* fieldstones.):

- Passive voice (choose when).
- Don't get hung up on a title.
- Stop with the editing already.

My fieldstones tend to be a few words, so I remember what I was thinking. Fieldstones have one role: they remind you of what you want to write about some time in the future. That means fieldstones are not supposed to be perfect.

Fieldstones worked for me for a long time. Then I realized I had "too many" ideas to write about.

So I added the notion of an "idea bank" for me. I might want to write about any of these ideas at some point. I don't have to—I can. The ideas are options.

My idea bank tends to be themes for my writing:

- Product leadership.
- Everything about a nonfiction book.
- Adaptable leadership.

When I look at all these possibilities, I realize I have more ideas. For example, when should teams use product leadership? When should they not? What is a product leader? What kinds of characteristics does that person have? When should a product leader rule and get overruled?

That's what a "theme" is for me. Will I write about all of those ideas? Maybe. It depends on what I choose to write next.

For several years, I tried to organize my ideas and fieldstones into some semblance of order. I ended up wasting time and energy, so I no longer do that. I leave all my fieldstones and ideas in one electronic application. You might prefer index cards. If you only write one idea on each card, you won't feel like you're tied into an order.

Both too few or too many ideas can paralyze writers. When you freewrite your fieldstones and ideas, you can decide what to choose next.

The reality is that I can't tell the difference between anything in my idea bank and my fieldstones. However, the fact that I call them two things means I can add anything of any length. I don't have to have a phrase to add a fieldstone.

I always have a place to start writing.

Feel free to change those fieldstones and ideas as you review them. If I choose something and I realize I want a different perspective, I can do that. I don't have to worry about having the exact perfect fieldstone or idea to start writing.

Since I always have some words as fieldstones, and ideas in my idea bank, I never face the blank page problem. I always have some idea of what to write.

Here's how I create my idea bank and fieldstones:

- Choose a place to put all your ideas and stones. Some writers like index cards. I use the Notes app on my Mac, which syncs between all my electronic devices. I recommend someplace easy for you to access almost anywhere. That place is your bank.
- Deposit some notes into your bank. Here's how: take a couple of minutes to think about what you want to write. Now, write down all those ideas, one idea or stone to an index card or a note. If you like outlining, consider writing every outline

entry on a different card or note. Or if you prefer to mind map, add each leaf as a card or note. Postpone deciding on how to frame something you haven't written yet.
- Update your bank. The more I deposit into my idea bank, the more ideas I have. I might see something on social media, a question from a talk I gave, or a comment on a blog post. As I see or hear these ideas, I add them to my bank. Consider how you will do the same.

Here's how I think of my bank: I invest a little time to write down a fieldstone or an idea. When I'm ready to write, I can take something out of my bank. And even if I take it out, I don't have to throw it away once I used it. I might want to use that same idea or fieldstone for a different ideal reader.

What If You Forget to Write Down a Fieldstone?

Early in my writing career, I thought I needed to write every idea or fieldstone down because I might "lose" a good idea. Then I realized how often I wrote similar ideas down.

The good ideas come around again. I recommend you write them down as they occur to you. That way, you feel comfortable writing down something as small as one word and as long as a paragraph. But don't worry about losing ideas. The more you write, the more ideas you will have to write.

Every so often I look in my bank and realize I have several related fieldstones. Now, I have choices. I might use all of them for one article. Or, I might use one each, in a series of articles. Or, I might use different ideal readers and focus on one fieldstone for each reader.

Because I capture all these ideas in one place, I can always choose what to write and when.

My idea bank and fieldstones are options or starting points. I can choose one of them as is. Or I can choose one and modify it in some way. Or, I can choose something entirely different. My idea bank prevents the blank problem.

And, I always have something that interests me that I can write about.

2.2 Write What Interests You

With any luck, you added ideas that interest you to your idea bank and fieldstones. If you *have* to write something for work, can you think about a way to approach that topic that does interest you? That approach will likely interest your readers, too.

That means any idea from your bank or fieldstones will *interest* you. You won't have to worry about a blank page if you write what interests you.

If you start with what interests you, you'll enjoy thinking and learning as you write. That assumes you're writing from your experience and expertise.

And if you realize you're no longer interested in these topics? Change, add more fieldstones, and move to other topics.

Consider these questions as writing prompts to identify what interests you.:

- What do your readers need to know that you can explain? How can you use your expertise to explain what you know in detail? Consider what you would have loved to know "back then," your hard-won experience. That's the "write what you know" advice.
- Where do you want to clarify ideas you know? If you've offered talks about this topic, consider clarifying your ideas in writing. Every time I do this, I understand what I know and where I still learn.

- What do you want to explore? I write both expertise-driven and personal essays to explore what I want to learn more about.

Don't bother with trying to identify your writing "passion." If you're like me, the more you write, the more ideas you have and the more you want to write.

The more I consider these options of what to write about, the more exciting my writing becomes to me. Often, that means my writing becomes more exciting to my readers.

And if you realize your writing bores you, rethink how you will choose what to write next. Don't stick with "write what you know," when your brain says, "Learn this!" Worse, your readers will see your boredom and stop reading.

Now that you always have a topic, you can pick something to write fast.

I encourage you to write fast. In fact, the faster you write, the more likely you are to learn and be able to make your writing even better. In addition, you'll reinforce your author voice.

However, you can't learn from your writing if you don't finish your pieces.

2.3 Finish What You Start

When I first started to write, I had a number of articles not quite done. That was back before I changed my writing rules.

I had trouble finishing any of the articles, often because I wasn't sure how to structure a piece. Only looming deadlines made me finish anything. (See Chapter 4 for structures that will help you finish your writing.)

I also have the "finishing energy" problem. I have a ton of starting energy because I love to think and learn as I write. Once I see where the piece is going, I sometimes get bored when it's time to finish. (Yes, my structures help me maintain finishing energy, too.)

Add to that, the slower I write, the less energy I have to finish. I feel as if I'm stuck, on this piece and any other pieces.

I created a writing rule about finishing that works for me: "I must finish what I start unless something catastrophic happens."

If you have rules about making your writing perfect as opposed to rules about finishing it, See Chapter 7 for a deeper discussion of rules. Or, if you're worried about how other people will judge you, reread the fear section in Chapter 1.

However, there's a better reason to finish what you start. The longer you take to finish, the longer the piece takes.

 Everything takes longer than you think it will.

As a project manager, I knew about Murphy's Law: "Everything that can go wrong, will. Often at the worst possible time." I also knew about Hofstadter's Law: It always takes longer than you expect, even when you take into account Hofstadter's Law[1].

It turns out that they were right, but incomplete. The more work you have in progress, the longer everything takes. Your throughput goes down. Little's Law explains this with numbers[2].

If you, like me, have limited writing time, finish what you start, as quickly as possible. Use your idea bank and fieldstones to "park" incomplete work that occurred to you as you wrote. Finish one piece at a time.

Imagine you think a 500-word blog post should take you about thirty minutes to write, and another five minutes to find the artwork

---

[1] "Gödel, Escher, Bach: An Eternal Golden Braid. 20th anniversary ed., 1999.
[2] https://www.jrothman.com/mpd/2022/03/littles-law-for-any-kind-of-product-development-how-to-learn-how-long-your-work-will-take/

for it. You start to write. But, ten minutes later the phone rings. You stop writing to answer the phone. After the call, you have a bunch of other work and you don't return to that piece for a couple of days.

You review what you wrote then and what you think now, are not the same. You have a different focus. So you restart the piece—and you realize it's now something different. You have two pieces of writing in progress.

And, you only have ten minutes today, so you put that piece down, too.

If you continue this for a couple of weeks, you have five or six pieces in progress. You've been writing, but you have nothing to show for it. How do you feel?

If you're like most people, you feel frustrated you didn't finish anything. You've spent time but no one else can read any of the pieces.

That's why I recommend you start and finish as fast as possible. The faster you write *and finish* the more energy and passion your readers will see in your work. And you won't feel as if you have a lot of writing hanging over your head, following you to all your other work.

If you have the problem of too many in-progress and unfinished pieces, choose one piece. Finish it. If you realize you have other ideas, add those to your fieldstones. Finish that first piece and write fast to do so. That piece might be short—which is fine.

When you write fast—and with passion—you can free your inner writer.

That means I want to shorten the feedback loop between what I think and what I write. The shorter that feedback loop, the faster I write and the better the result. I can choose something to write (the start of the feedback loop), write without editing or stopping for fifteen minutes, cycle to finish, and then publish (the end of the feedback loop).

In Chapter 1, I said nonfiction writers write-to-think *and* think-to-write. We do that by cycling over the piece.

2.4 Cycle for Clarity

When you tried the freewriting activity, you wrote your words, always moving forward. Since I also said I iterate, you might wonder how. That's the cycling part. Cycling helps me learn what I think and refine what I write next.

First, I write down, focused on one valuable chunk. After those fifteen minutes, I reread what I wrote. I often discover I need to clarify the logic and add more details. I plan just enough to start a new writing timebox. I don't try to edit as I go.

That's my writing process, as you can see in this next figure.

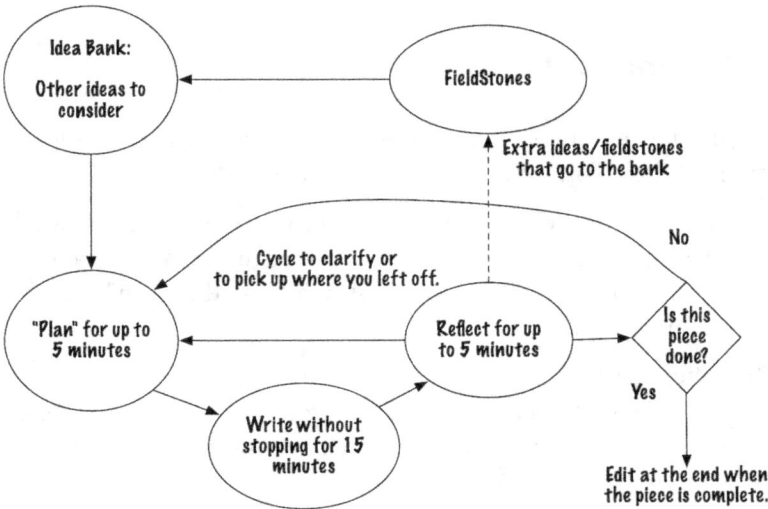

Figure 2.1: My Writing Process

My writing process is a reinforcing feedback loop to keep me in writing-down mode. I plan just enough, write down, reflect, and cycle until I'm done.

The more you stay in writing and cycling to integrate what you think and learn, the more you can maintain your momentum. Now let's see in more detail how to write fast and well.

2.5 See How to Write Fast and Well

Here's a walkthrough of how to free your inner nonfiction writer.

2.5.1 Select an Idea

You've looked through your idea bank and selected an idea or a fieldstone as a starting point. If you have not yet created your idea bank, select an idea from the freewriting activity in Chapter 1.

Now, use a title to focus your ideas.

2.5.2 Focus With a Title

If you have a ton of ideas, you might not know where to start. A title will help you focus on one or several tightly related ideas.

Sometimes, I start with a horrible title. I choose a fieldstone as a title, or a key idea. Most of the time, I recommend you avoid spending any time making this title "good." Instead, use this "bad" title as a focus for your piece.

Too often, writers spend time writing the perfect title—and realize that title goes with a different piece. Avoid that time trap and start to write. See how to refine the title when you're done, in Chapter 4.

Every so often, I take the time to create a wonderful title. If I have several possible readers, I use the title analyzers in Chapter 4 to test my titles. Those tests can change my perspective on the piece. However, I don't spend more than five minutes testing a great title. I write, rather than title. I recommend you do the same.

Here's how I start with a "bad" title. Imagine I plan to write an article about how project managers should use stories to explain status. I write: "Use stories to explain status" as the title, at the top of the document.

That's a terrible title in many ways. However, it serves one purpose: that title will focus my writing. I won't write anything else—I'll just write about that topic.

Now, given that title, use your title as a focus to decide which problems you'll address in this article.

2.5.3 Decide Which Problems to Write About

Nonfiction educates, persuades, and entertains readers. That means we start with problems.

Consider this question: "What does the ideal reader need to know about this topic that they don't already know?" I'll talk more about the ideal reader in Chapter 3. For now, think of a real person who has this problem.

I met a skeptical guy, whom I'll call Terry, many years ago. Terry offered me terrific feedback on my writing. "I see what you say, but I don't believe you. I need more examples to believe you."

Now, as I write, I ask myself what Terry might say. That helps me empathize with Terry and his concerns.

If you like outlines or mind maps, you might normally start with one. I hope you won't. Outlines or mind maps shortcut your thinking and learning because they only include what you already know—your synthesis of the ideas. More often, writers need to add insights that they can see only when they think and learn.

If you normally do think with an outline or a mind map avoid starting with those tools for your next three articles. You might realize, as I have, that outlines or mind maps are excellent diagnostic tools after I start to write, not before.

> ## Why Shouldn't I Start with an Outline?
>
> If you know everything you need to know about this topic, sure, start with an outline. I'm not the outline police. However, if you can avoid a starting outline, you might realize you make connections as you write, connections you didn't make before.
>
> Give your brain the space to think and learn as you write. Use the outline as a diagnostic tool to check your logic once you're done writing. Or, if you don't know where to go from here, use the outline as a diagnostic tool to consider your options. See how to structure your piece in Chapter 3 for more alternatives.

What if you're not sure what the reader needs to know? Go meta, to think about the problem that caused you to write this idea. Write about *that* problem.

Here's an example. I had a fieldstone that said, "multitasking is so terrible for human beings." I've already written articles and books about multitasking problems. What is the problem I want to address now?

This time, as I go meta, I realize I want to write about people and their courage to say the word No as a complete sentence.

I didn't realize that's what I wanted to write about when I wrote the fieldstone. I started to write to learn why I wanted to write about that. I had to go meta to realize the point of the article.

Now, it's time to write forward.

2.5.4 Write Forward for Fifteen Minutes

Set a timer for fifteen minutes and write.

I write, keeping Terry in mind. Terry isn't always my ideal reader, but he is a stand-in for many of my ideal readers. Terry reminds me to add concrete details to my piece.

As you write, ask yourself what do your readers need to know? See Chapter 3 for more discussion of ideal readers. For now, write forward across the page.

What if you realize you mistyped a word? If you must, return and fix that—under one condition. If you start to rearrange or replace words, you're editing. Avoid that. Consider not looking at the page while you write, so you can continue to write forward. Otherwise, ignore your typos for now.

You will learn what you think if you keep your fingers or pen moving across the page. That will allow you to write more than you realize and make connections you didn't see before. Allow yourself to learn as you write.

When your timer goes off, decide if you want to finish your last sentence. (Some writers leave that last sentence unfinished. I hate doing that, so I finish the sentence.)

If you're like many writers, you'll write about 300 words in about fifteen minutes. Then it's time to cycle.

2.5.5 Cycle At About Fifteen Minutes

Since we think and learn as we write, we need to cycle to integrate what we learned. For many nonfiction writers, that cyle time is about fifteen minutes, or about 200-400 words.

When I cycle, I reread to understand:

- Logic: Does this piece make sense? As you integrate your thinking and learning, do the early words still make sense where they are?
- Flow: Is the information in the place where the reader needs it?
- Meaning: You might need to choose different words, especially if you learned from your writing.

What if you're only finishing 100 words every fifteen minutes? You haven't written enough to clarify your logic, flow, or meaning.

In that case, diagnose why you're writing slowly:

- Are you writing in a language that's not your native language? You will be slower than my guidelines.
- You're not sure what to write next. Consider taking a quick stretch or water break. Alternatively, consider a different reader and then restart this piece. Put the original piece in your fieldstones.
- You're editing old words, not creating new words. I see this reason most often. Do not interrupt yourself with editing. Wait to edit until you're done.

Only you know the answer to why you're writing more slowly than you can. If you're not sure what to write next, think about what this reader needs to know. See more information in Chapter 3.

Remember, writing creates new words.

Let's assume you do write roughly 200-400 words in fifteen minutes. Now it's time to back up a little to integrate your thinking and learning. To do that, read from where you started to write, and see what you might want to consider next. Even before you formally reflect, acknowledge what you learned. You might have more ideas to integrate. Or, you might want to analyze or apply two or three new ideas you didn't have before.

If you have a ton of new ideas, consider writing sticky notes, one with each idea, and putting that note off to the side. Or, add those ideas to your bank.

I cycle best when I write clean and maintain my momentum. You can too. If you cycle, you don't need multiple drafts where you might tempt yourself to rewrite the entire piece.

For example, I excel at writing one large idea in one sentence. When I cycle, I realize Terry needs more information. That's when I expand the one large idea into the entire paragraph of information I missed the first time. I'm not rewriting or creating a new draft. I'm clarifying what I just wrote, so Terry can understand.

Cycling allows you to assess the clarity of your ideas, not the correctness of the words or the sentences. Editing helps you correct words and sentences.

Here are clarifications you might add as you cycle:

- Examples, stories, or anecdotes that clarify the piece for your ideal reader.
- Additional ideas, because you thought and learned as you wrote.
- Subheadings so the reader can follow the text more clearly.

Here's an example of what I mean by a story or anecdote:

> "When Harry started to write, he had big honking paragraphs of seven, eight, nine sentences. Each sentence was at least twenty words long. The first feedback I offered was to add more paragraphs. Then, I asked him to add more periods, to write shorter sentences. Just that small feedback helped him write better and faster."

Let me go meta and explain that example. With any luck, you've seen writing like that and tried to puzzle your way through it.

Harry had great ideas, but he buried those ideas in large and long paragraphs. Once Harry made more paragraphs, he saw where to add more details. And when he changed his sentence length, he realized what else he needed to write.

I fictionalized that example, because I have yet to offer feedback to anyone named Harry. However, the story is based on real people and their experiences.

Readers like to see the concreteness that examples, stories, and anecdotes offer. Even if you structure your writing to a specific template, see if you can add specific examples.

As you cycle, you might take the chance to reflect on what you wrote.

2.5.6 Reflect on What You Wrote

Sometimes, in nonfiction, we need to research something so we're ready for the next piece of writing. This is an excellent time to plan and organize your ideas for your next writing down session.

I don't tend to spend a lot of time reflecting, because I do that as I cycle. If I have stickies from cycling, I might use this time to decide if they go into this piece or into my bank.

If you're ready to continue writing, do continue. However, if you don't have more time right now, save what you're doing. You'll be ready to pick up again here.

2.5.7 Continue to Write Forward

If you have the available time, continue to write just after you cycle. I still recommend you cycle for clarity every fifteen minutes.

As soon as you're done, that's when you can edit.

2.5.8 Edit at the End

See Chapter 4 for a full discussion of editing. In the meantime, remember that your first job as a writer is to explain your ideas well. Only try to correct your writing after you clarify your ideas.

If you're not a great speller, consider checking your spelling first, before anything else.

You've seen the whole writing forward process now. You can maintain your momentum even if you need several sessions to finish your piece. Learn to write clean to maintain your momentum.

2.6 Write Clean to Maintain Momentum

I like to maintain my momentum as I write. That means I write as clean as I can. I already discussed how cycling helps clarify my logic, flow, and meaning.

Sometimes, I write a paragraph or two and when I reread, I don't understand what I wrote. In that case, I review the paragraph and ask myself what did I want to help the reader understand? That's the gem in that paragraph.

I take that idea, that gem, and delete the original paragraph. Then, I start over with a new paragraph. I stay in writing-down, writing forward. I rarely try to fix a paragraph.

 Sometimes, it's easier to delete a paragraph rather than fix it.

You might worry—will you slow yourself down if you throw out sentences and paragraphs as you cycle? When I keep the gem and throw out the original words, I gain speed. My original paragraph told me what I thought. I learned what I wanted to say in that original paragraph. It's much easier to rewrite rather than fix. So starting fresh allows me to gain speed.

When Should You Toss a Piece?

Sometimes, you finish writing something and you think, "This stinks." You decide to delete it.

Before you toss it out, consider these other options: put it away until tomorrow; put it back in your fieldstones.

If you write at the end of the day, as I often do, I think everything stinks. That's because I'm tired and frustrated with my seeming inability to say what I think. If I read it the next day, I often realize I have said what I thought. Or, I find the gems in that piece and can rewrite it the next day. And it won't take me that long to rewrite because I already did the hard work of thinking and learning.

Maybe you wrote first thing in the morning and you still don't think you did a good job. You might be too harsh on yourself. Finish this piece and ask a trusted friend or colleague to read it. Ask the question, "Did I lose you anywhere?" (See Chapter 5 for more discussion about feedback.) Listen to that person. Then, you can decide what to do.

Sometimes, you don't say what you mean. I recognize that when I start to shake my head and laugh at what I wrote. I recommend you put that writing—as is—into a folder called "Bad starts" or something like that. Then, in a *new* document, rewrite the piece so you write what you want to say. Don't allow your old writing to influence your new words.

I always start with rereading what I wrote in the last chunk of writing. At the very end, when I think I'm done, I reread from the start.

As I write and cycle, I check my logic, flow, and meaning. Then, at the end, I can see how everything flows together.

I know that several famous writers advocate you "vomit" words onto the page. Or that you write a "shitty" first draft. (See *Bird by Bird: Some Instructions On Writing and Life* LAM07. The difference between my suggestions to write clean and cycle is that they recommend you write "dirty." I would rather find my flow to write.

Why would you think of your writing as vomit or shit? Why not create a system for you that helps you see the gems in your writing?

You are an expert with valuable ideas to share. You have gems. Write those gems, and keep your writing clean.

You might need to practice spelling to write clean.

2.7 Practice Correct Spelling

Part of writing clean is your ability to spell, so you don't go back to fix typos. And I recommended you turn off the spell-checker and grammar checker as you write, so you don't edit as you write.

What do you do about those typos? Aside from not looking at the screen as you proceed, consider these alternatives:

- Dictate your writing and let the dictation program spell correctly.
- Get a text expansion program and learn how to use it.
- As you cycle, fix your spelling for clarity. Not for perfection.

The whole idea is to maintain your writing momentum and edit at the very end of your piece.

2.8 Practice Writing Faster to Write Well

How can you be ready to write fast and well? Consider these ideas.

1. Choose a place for your idea bank. If you didn't add ideas or fieldstones yet, write at least ten or twelve of them now. You can then avoid the blank page problem.
2. As you write forward, start to learn when you need to cycle through the piece. Do you need to cycle every two hundred words? Maybe you can wait for five hundred words. As you cycle, make sure you explain the problems and solutions to yourself, first.
3. Wait to edit until you finish writing "all" the words. Editing interrupts your thinking and learning. Editing kills your writing.
4. Try several fifteen-minute timeboxes to write an entire article or blog post, all the way through. Edit after you're all done, and then see what you think about your writing.

The more you practice writing fast, the easier the writing is.

Now that you've practiced writing fast, let's discuss how to draw your ideal reader into your piece.

3. Write for Your Ideal Reader

Do you know your ideal reader? If you're like me, you might write for several kinds of readers at different times. However, each piece has one ideal reader. Other readers might benefit, but aim each piece at one kind of reader.

How can you do that? Start with empathy.

3.1 Empathize with Your Readers

Consider this: Your readers are unaware of your perspective or information. Or they want to understand something important. That's why you write—to share your experience and expertise with these people.

That means that readers might ask ignorant questions. However, most readers are not intentionally stupid, bad, or wrong. They are unaware. That's why I recommend you empathize with these people.

What about the readers who vehemently disagree with you? I like to think about them as people with different data. Their experience does not match mine. Maybe they cannot imagine my perspective, even though I offered examples. Or, they might just want to pick a fight with me.

There are always readers who disagree with you or tell you you're wrong. That's fine. While your information might be correct, they might not be able to accept or understand it yet. Or, they cannot imagine you might be correct.

However, most readers want to understand your information. They want you to educate, influence, and entertain them.

The more you empathize with these readers, the more likely you are to reach them. Maybe not the first time they read your writing, but if they keep reading what you write, you will reach them. Eventually. You can grab their attention and keep them in the piece.

If you ever start to blame, ridicule, or mock your readers, stop writing *this* piece. Instead, write for yourself about why you want to insult your readers. This is an example of going meta, writing about why the problem exists, instead of the problem itself. You might realize you need to write for a different reader.

What about satire or parody? In my experience, there's a fine line between satire and mocking the very people you want to reach. Some readers might even experience the satire as blame, ridicule, or condescension.

Write what you want. Then, decide if the piece offers the value to your ideal reader.

Use your empathy to write about what matters to your readers.

3.2 Write About What Matters

When you identify what matters to your ideal reader, you answer the "So What" question. How do you know what matters? Consider the problems your readers need to solve. Write about those.

Here are three ideas to understand the "so what" question:

- What problems do people speak with you about? Or, what problems do you see?
- What questions do people ask you to solve?
- When your readers need to make decisions, what questions do they ask?

All of those questions might help you see what matters to your ideal readers.

When we write nonfiction, we often want to influence people to consider alternatives, or make reasoned decisions. Writers help the decision-maker see the problems and the effect of those problems on other people.

 Answer the "So What" question for your readers.

Imagine you can't leave a review online for a product you bought. Let's eavesdrop on the internal written conversation between the software person and the manager who decides what to do next. Remember that there is a time delay of at least an hour between these pieces of writing:

Software person generates a problem report: "We need to fix the pop-up for the reviews. It's not working. Customers are complaining."

Manager writes: "Can they still leave a review?"

Software person replies: "Sometimes. But it's inconvenient."

Manager: "Leave it for later."

The initial problem report did not describe what matters, the "so what," to their managers.

Instead, what if the second half of the conversation starting with "sometimes" went this way:

Software person: "Sometimes. With our most recent changes, we made it inconvenient for most reviewers to leave reviews. That's because we changed how the browser works. Since we made those changes, we've noticed 50% fewer reviews each month. We know reviews—positive or negative—drive buying. I wonder if we lose potential customers if we don't fix it."

Manager: "Oh, that's bad. We want more customers and more revenue. Fine, go and fix it."

In this case, the "so what" is about customer ease of use, attracting future customers, and revenue. If you know why this issue or problem matters to your ideal reader, you can write to inform them.

I know of three primary ways to frame what matters to your ideal readers:

- Risks, current concerns. Risks tend to use "away from" language, things the ideal reader does not want.
- Benefits, possibilities for future growth. Benefits tend to use "toward" language, what the reader does want.
- Options to consider as the reader weighs your arguments.

All of these possibilities can educate or influence your ideal reader. Let's start with risks.

3.2.1 Reframe Risks

In their classic *Strategic Selling: The Unique Sales System Proven Successful by America's Best Companies* MIH85, Miller and Heiman use the idea of helping people see the discrepancy between their current reality and the possible future. The person might have trouble—risks, or might have growth opportunities—benefits.

Let's start with risks.

In the earlier vignette about the ability to leave reviews on a site, the second explanation focuses on the risks of leaving the software as is. The writer wrote about ease of use, the need for more reviews, and the risks of losing potential customers.

Notice that the writer did not write, "You were wrong in your previous decision." Very few people ever want to admit they're wrong. Instead, focus on the how the current situation will influence the future.

Part of that focus might be for you to discuss what the ideal reader will lose. Consider both tangible and intangible costs. For example, in the software problem report above, the software person might add, "The sales before we made this change were x, and last quarter, after the change, they were y."

Intangible costs might include customer ease of use or goodwill.

Risks have implicit costs. You might need to make them explicit, with away-from language.

Once you explain the risks, discuss what matters with benefits.

3.2.2 Show Benefits

Benefits allow you to show the ideal reader possible growth opportunities—a vision of the future.

Show, with anecdotes, stories, and data how the reader might benefit. Your ideas might:

- Save the reader money or time.
- Create new opportunities for the reader or their customers.
- Make their work or lives easier in some way.

Assume that your readers are unaware of the benefits. Otherwise, they would have already put your ideas into practice. Introduce the ideas so the reader can say, "Aha! Now I understand."

Sometimes, you don't need people to change—but you do want them to consider more options, so they can be more flexible. You can choose either away-from or toward language for options.

3.2.3 Consider Options

Help the reader realize there are more options, not necessarily based on risks or benefits.

Not all nonfiction requires that people change. Sometimes, we want people to consider a different perspective or other options.

Personal essays are an example of writing that tends to ask people to reconsider their actions or beliefs without asking for the reader to change. Personal essays offer insight from the writer's experience and perspective. Writers offer those insights freely, without asking for the reader to change.

All three of these ideas—risks, benefits, options—invite your readers into your writing. When you write about what matters and speak your reader's language, the reader is ready for what you propose.

One more thing about what matters: see if you can offer your reader three options for what matters when you write.

3.3 Organize with the Rule of Three

You might have noticed something about this book: I often use three options for lists. And when you see subheadings, you'll see three pieces of content.

I used the Rule of Three as an example to show you how you might organize your writing. For example, you might want to offer three risks, benefits,or options in a given piece. Or, you might want to offer two benefits and one risk.

What's so great about the Rule of Three?

- People see patterns when you offer three items[1].
- Most of us can only remember three items at a time.
- In addition, I follow Weinberg's Rule of Three: *If you can't think of three things that might go wrong with your plans, then there's something wrong with your thinking* from Weinberg's *The Secrets of Consulting* WCO14.

---

[1] https://www.inc.com/bill-murphy-jr/how-rule-of-3-makes-people-listen-better-remember-more-understand-what-you-have-to-say.html

Writers and consultants have a lot in common. We offer alternatives for our readers, to rethink how they work or live. When writers offer multiple alternatives, readers are more likely to believe the writer. Especially if writers use Weinberg's Rule of Three in this way:

- One alternative is a trap.
- Two alternatives is a false choice—a dilemma.
- Three alternatives offer a real choice. In addition, it's a way to create more alternatives.

What about more than three options? Are more than three options useful?

Maybe.

People don't remember much, even when they read a relatively short piece of writing. Most people can remember three items according to *George Miller's Magical Number of Immediate Memory in Retrospect: Observations on the Faltering Progression of Science* COW16. A few people can remember four items.

However, you might overwhelm your reader when you offer more than three options[2]. If you have more than three options, consider how you might organize all those ideas into a series.

Instead of lots of options in one piece, offer your ideal reader three alternatives and make each alternative matter to them.

And, if you have a distinct choice, be honest about that choice, instead of trying to drive your reader to *your* choice.

Now, use everything you know about your reader and what matters to hook the reader with a problem.

---

[2]https://www.inc.com/bill-murphy-jr/the-us-marine-corps-uses-rule-of-3-to-organize-almost-everything-heres-how-learning-it-21-years-ago-changed-my-life.html

3.4 Hook The Reader with a Problem

People read nonfiction to see how they might solve problems. Start a piece by sharing the problem as a way to set the context, so the reader can see if this piece is for him or her.

Here are three ways to hook the reader with a problem:

- One Startling Sentence
- Hey! You! See! So!
- A story that shows someone similar to the ideal reader in a setting.

Each of these possibilities sets the context for the reader and invites the reader into your thinking.

Let's start with One Startling Sentence to invite the reader in.

3.4.1 One Startling Sentence

I no longer remember how or when I discovered Kent Beck's *One Startling Sentence*,[3] but I am thrilled I did.

One Startling Sentence consists of a four-sentence paragraph in this order:

- First sentence: What's the problem?
- Second sentence: Why is this problem a problem? (Note: this is what matters to the reader.)
- Third sentence: The startling sentence.
- Fourth sentence: Implication of the startling sentence.

Here's an example where my ideal reader is a technical leader, but not a senior manager. That reader works where she's supposed to multitask all the time.

---

[3] http://wiki.c2.com/?OneStartlingSentence

> "Are you a leader who's supposed to work on or with many teams? Too often, you feel as you get more behind every day instead of making progress. You don't have to fall behind—you can manage your personal project portfolio. Learn to show your boss(es) all your work and have the challenging "No" conversation."

The startling sentence is: "You don't have to fall behind—you can manage your personal project portfolio."

This opening is just one possibility. "Hey! You! See! So!" offers an alternative.

3.4.2 Hey! You! See! So!

I also don't remember when I learned this approach to an opening. A colleague whose writing I enjoyed explained it to me. He had learned it earlier—possibly from Gerald M. Weinberg.

Bob Dotson, the longtime journalist, discussed this in a video[4].

- *Hey!* get the reader to pay attention.
- *You!* is why the reader should care about this issue—what matters.
- *See?* is the one or two facts that you have—that no one else has.
- *So...* is why the reader should care.

Here's an alternative opening:

> "You have too much to do and you feel as if you're falling behind daily. But you can make progress once you convince your bosses that you *can't* do more work.

---
[4] https://youtu.be/K0Rp9kP8gVs

> You can visualize your work and have that No conversation with all those people who want you to do all that work. Then, you can get back to your normal productive self."

The "See?" is this sentence: "You can visualize your work and have that No conversation with all those people who want you to do all that work."

But, let's try the third alternative, to start with a story.

3.4.3 Start with a Story

One way to set the context is to help the reader see the issues through someone else's eyes. A story is a short anecdote, personalized with a fictitious person:

> "Trish, a project manager was so frustrated. She was supposed to manage three projects. But, every project needed more time than she had in any given day. She felt more and more behind and she had no idea if she could ever catch up. She'd heard of a way to visualize her work and say that big fat No to her managers. What did she have to lose?"

Those are just three possible openings, each of them aimed at one ideal reader. When it's time for you to write an opening, consider which one appeals to you more—for the specific piece you're writing.

Regardless of the type of piece you're writing—consider how you might use or adapt one of these openings. I've used all three openings, even for more formal writing. Choose an opening that will invite your ideal reader into your piece.

You don't have to get the opening perfect the first time you sit down to write. Write enough of the hook that you can set the context for yourself, not just the ideal reader. Then, as you write and cycle, return to the opening and refine it.

You might wonder if there are more than three ways to open a piece of writing. There are. There are as many ways as there are writers. However, I've offered you ways to see patterns to start with a problem. You can always choose to start differently.

Now that you have an opening, refine your logic to help your readers understand.

3.5 Structure Your Piece with Logic

Your job as a writer is to make your thoughts clear to your ideal reader. What does that reader need to know and when?

That's how you'll decide the structure of your piece.

I know of three satisfying structures for nonfiction writing:

- Algis Budrys' 7-point plot outline for fiction.
- What I'll call "Three Possibilities": An opening that draws readers in with what matters in the current state. Then, offer three actions, secrets, or tips. End with a summary of the new state that reminds the reader of the opening.
- Barbara Minto's Pyramid Principle, where you ask questions and answer them.

Don't worry about using a fiction structure for nonfiction. First, all nonfiction contains fiction and all fiction contains nonfiction. Second, many of your ideal readers won't believe your nonfiction even when it's true. You need to make some things up so your readers believe you.

Each structure allows me to check my logic in different ways.

3.5.1 Budrys' 7-Point Plot Outline

Algis Budrys publicized his seven-point plot outline for fiction:

Points 1, 2, 3: A character, in a situation, with a problem. These points set the context for the rest of the piece. I suggested that you hook the reader with a problem. Since you're either talking about a character or talking to your ideal reader, you now have a character, in a context, with a problem.

Points 4 and 5 are called "try/fail" cycles. In fiction, the protagonist tries something and fails. The fiction writer adds enough of these try/fail cycles to make the story interesting. For nonfiction, your ideal reader has a problem. Often, one alternative is not enough for the reader to solve the problem. That's why three ideas help the reader see even more alternatives, especially in their context.

Point 6 is the climax of the piece. When someone uses your solutions, this is how they succeed.

Point 7 is the validation. Since I suggest you finish the piece with a reminder of the opening, the reader feels satisfied.

> ## Experience Reports Follow Budrys' Outline
>
> Experience reports are a special type of nonfiction—they tell the story of how you succeeded or failed over a specific time. Start with the initial problem, including who that problem affected and why someone wanted to change. Then, continue with a chronological explanation of the solutions you tried. Include what worked and didn't work.
>
> Since experience reports bound the problem by time, include as many try/fail cycles as you need to tell the story. Regardless of whether you think you succeeded or failed, at the end of the report, remind your readers of the initial state you described

> in your opening. Include what everyone learned.
>
> Follow Budrys' outline and you'll write a satisfying experience report.

Here's an example of how I might close the article about multitasking:

"Trish leaned back in her chair and took a deep breath. She glanced at her board, thankful it had only five items total for just one team. She'd been honest and respectful to her boss, and he'd listened to her. Now it was time to get busy so she could help the team finish this project."

We know what happened and that the article is complete.

I didn't realize I used Budrys' outline until I checked it against my "Three Possibilities" approach.

3.5.2 Three Possibilities

I use the Three Possibilities structure often for blog posts, newsletters, articles—even book chapters.

Here's what Three Possibilities looks like:

1. Identify the current state, with any of the openings back in "Hook the Reader with a Problem."
2. Explain three possibilities in the form of tips, ideas, or approaches that will help the reader solve the problem(s) in the current state.
3. Finish the piece with a new state that helps the reader reflect back to the opening.

If I continue the Trish, the project manager opening, the three possibilities might be:

- Trish created a board to show all her work. That might have been enough to show her boss all the work she did.
- From experience, she was sure that board was not enough. However, exposing her work on a visual medium helped her prepare for a conversation with her boss.
- She considered several ways to say No without alienating her boss.

When you write this way, you deliver what matters to your ideal reader, using easy-to-follow logic. You can make the piece easier to follow when you add a subheading for each major idea.

What if you only have two possibilities? Add a third section explaining when your ideas won't work.

What if you have nine possibilities? Some possibilities:

- Write one article with three groups of three possibilities.
- Write three articles, each with one group of three.
- Write nine articles, treating each possibility separately.

Avoid overwhelming your readers. Instead, write more, shorter pieces.

But what if you've been thinking about your topic for a long time and you have many fieldstones or big ideas? You might need to organize those chunks in various ways. The Pyramid Principle might work for you.

3.5.3 The Pyramid Principle

When I started writing, I asked several friends for feedback on my articles. One of them said, "JR, you have *all* your ideas in this one article. I can't follow it. You need to separate some of them so I can read what you want to say."

Then he told me about Barbara Minto's *The Minto Pyramid Principle: Logic in Writing and Thinking* MIN87.

The Pyramid starts with this introduction:

- Situation: Define the current state.
- Complication: What's the change?
- Question: What's the hypothesis or questions we need to answer?
- Answer: State the solution.

This looks a little like One Startling Sentence to me.

Here's the opening paragraph if we use Trish, the multitasking project manager, as an example:

"Trish, along with all the other project managers, attempts to manage several projects at a time. None of them feel successful because they're all multitasking all the time. Instead of multitasking, they need a way to choose which work to do and which work to stop for now. They will use kanban boards and limit their work in progress."

Here's a pyramid for Trish and her multitasking problem:

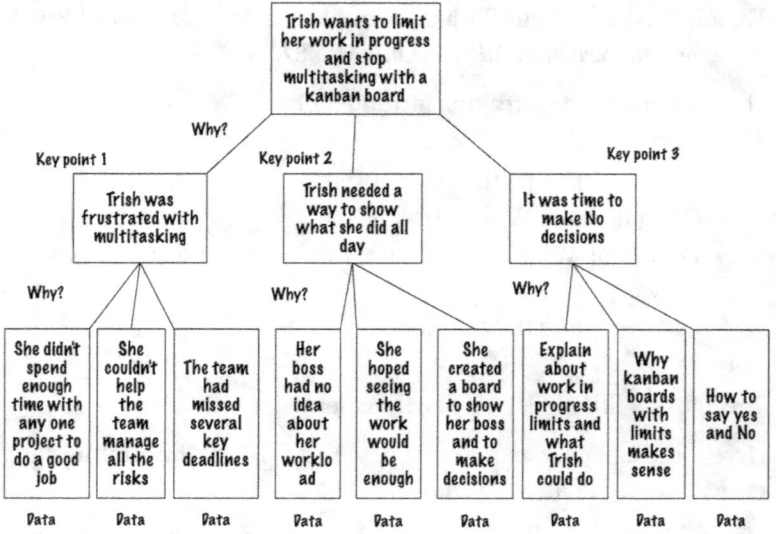

Figure 3.1 Pyramid Principle

The top box has the initial SCQA: "Trish wants to limit her work in progress and stop multitasking with a kanban board."

The situation is: Trish is multitasking. The complication (the change) is: stop multitasking. The question (hypothesis) is: will that help Trish finish the work? The answer is: use a kanban board with work in progress limits.

Every horizontal box is a Key Point and answers the why question from the box above it. The key points on the bottom use data to support the box above.

Keep the horizontal boxes roughly parallel in detail.

You might wonder why I suggest the Pyramid Principle if I don't suggest outlining or mindmapping. The Pyramid Principle is a way for you to think and learn as you fill out the boxes. Or, if you're like me, you can use it to diagnose any logic problems in your final piece.

The Pyramid Principle invites you to think and learn as you proceed.

You don't need all the answers in advance. As long as you continue with Situation, Complication, Question, Answer, you will think and learn as you proceed.

If you have many fieldstones—or many ideas—the Pyramid Principle might help you organize both the logic and the structure for *this* piece. If anyone suggests they don't understand your logic, consider the Pyramid Principle structure your piece.

And if you're still worried about your outline or mind map, I'll discuss those as diagnostic tools in Chapter 4.

Now it's time to finish by reminding your reader of how you started the piece.

3.6 End With a Reminder of the Start

How can you write a satisfying ending? By reminding the reader of how you started.

If you started with One Startling Sentence, remind your reader of the startling sentence. If you used the Hey structure, remind them of the See, the one or two unique pieces of information. If you started with a story, write another paragraph about the person, and how that person used the ideas in this piece.

Now that you know all the pieces: the problem, the logic, and a satisfying ending, write the piece in any order you like.

3.7 Write In Any Order

Although I explained in reading order, you don't have to write from the top of the piece down.

Some writers start with one of their key ideas, and spiral in and out, refining as they write. They stay in writing-down mode, and do not edit.

Some writers start from the top and write down in the same order the reader reads the piece. They are not afraid to reorder as they write and cycle.

I know of several writers who seem to know the end, but not how to get there. They start with their conclusion and work backward, often using a structure similar to the Pyramid Principle.

Don't worry about the order in which you write. Keep writing and cycling so you integrate your learning and thinking as you proceed. Continue to educate, influence, and entertain your reader as you write.

3.8 Practice Writing for Your Ideal Reader

You've seen many alternatives in this chapter. Now it's your turn to practice.

1. Select one idea or fieldstone from your idea bank.
2. Choose an ideal reader for this piece.
3. Decide what matters to that reader. Use that to frame your hook.
4. Maintain your 15-minute timeboxes and cycle:
    - Start your piece with a problem to invite your ideal reader into your writing.
    - Structure your piece. Consider how you will use the Rule of Three and how you will write about what matters to your reader. Add subheadings so the reader can see your logic.
    - Make sure your ending reminds readers of the start.
5. Avoid editing. Continue to write forward.

If you can't write for an hour at a time, don't worry. Use your 15-minute timeboxes to finish roughly 200-300 words in each timebox—even if you have to use several days to finish this piece. Make sure you cycle as you write, especially if you need several days to finish this piece.

If you catch yourself editing, congratulate yourself on noticing and continue to write forward and cycle.

Now that you have a piece of finished writing, it's time to discuss editing.

4. Edit Just Enough

You wrote and cycled through a piece of writing, focusing on your ideal reader and what that reader needs to know and when. You're ready to edit.

When you edit, you make your piece more accessible to your ideal reader. That's it. Not perfection, because there is no such thing as perfect writing. Use your edit time to focus on helping your reader understand what you convey through your writing.

Hopefully, I persuaded you to wait until you're done writing to edit. If you waited, you now see that:

- Cycling allows you to integrate your thinking and learning as you proceed.
- You don't need multiple drafts.
- Editing as you proceed shortcuts your thinking and learning, making everything take longer.

Writing nonfiction based on your expertise and experience is totally different from synthesizing other people's ideas.

Let's start with how you might decide when to edit.

4.1 Edit When You're Still Interested

Many well-meaning people offer this editing advice: put the piece aside for a while. Then, when you're no longer passionate about the work, edit.

I asked many of those people how long should I wait. Some people said, "at least a day, sometimes a month, maybe even a year." I thought that was nuts.

One kind soul said, "Until you're clear-headed and not passionate about the piece." When I said, "But I'm always passionate about this topic!" the other person shrugged.

That answer assumes that clear-headed is somehow different from passion. With any luck, you've seen through this book that you can be *both* clear-headed and passionate about your writing.

When I asked these people why I should postpone finishing to be more clear-headed, no one had an answer.

Instead, edit while you're still interested. Make it easy for you to finish and publish. (Even if "publish" means "send the memo via email.")

Let me explain a little about finishing energy. While I have plenty of starting energy, I hate to finish. I write a lot to practice finishing. To finish books and other longer writing, I create checklists because I have very little finishing energy. I wrote the thing. Why do I have to return to it?

If you're like me, you might put the piece aside and *never* return to it. I'm no longer interested in mostly-finished work. And that means I won't publish it because it's not done.

Why not edit and publish as soon as you're done writing and cycling?

Maybe you have the discipline to put a piece away and return to it. But I don't want to need discipline for any part of the writing process. I want to let my inner writer fly free.

Edit as soon as you think you're done writing.

If your editing causes you to think and learn, return to writing forward and cycling. Use that new thinking to write and cycle, continuing to integrate your thinking and learning as you proceed.

What if you finished your piece and you have no more writing time today? Edit at the start of your next writing time. Don't wait too long to edit, or you might never publish.

Now that you're ready to edit, ask yourself this question: "How little can I edit and keep my voice in the piece?"

4.2 Maintain Your Author Voice

You've been talking since you were two years old. You've been writing since you were seven or eight or so. That's a long time.

Each of us has a unique speaking and writing style. Some nonfiction writers have similar speaking and writing styles. Some writers have quite distinct styles for each.

What you sound like on paper—that's your author voice. The less you edit, the more you leave your author voice intact.

The stronger your author voice, the more the reader can see your passion and interest in your writing. Your readers can see why you're so interested in this topic. That interest draws them in.

You discover your author voice as you write and cycle, think and learn. Your voice might change depending on the type of nonfiction you write, but you will discover your voice.

I knew I found my voice when I met a colleague in real life. I'm five feet tall on a good day. He looked at me and said, "You write much taller than you are." (I do!)

When you discover your author voice, you'll attract people who read what you write because *you* wrote it. Those people don't worry about whether you used correct grammar. They care about almost any topic because you wrote it.

One way to maintain your author voice is to edit as little as possible.

4.3 Edit as Little as Possible

How much editing are you accustomed to doing? When I ask writers who still edit as they write, they often tell me they spend hours editing. Or they write several drafts of a 500-word blog post, editing after each draft.

If you feel the need to edit that much, consider cycling instead. Then, edit at the end.

Editing has several parts:

- The language part, where you'll correct spelling, choose words, and simplify your language. Also, balance your author voice with any language changes.
- The logic part, where you'll check that readers can follow your writing.
- Finalize your title to make sure the title fits your piece and attracts readers.

Keep this guideline in mind: start with the technical changes, such as spelling, and move to your style. However, most spelling checkers integrate grammar checking, too. That means that even the "technical" changes affect your author voice.

Start with the "technical" parts of editing: spelling, readability, and punctuation.

4.3.1 Always Check Spelling

Back in Chapter 1, I suggested you only fix spelling for clarity. Now, once you finish writing and cycling, turn the spell-checker on. Check all the spelling in your piece.

Some spell-checkers will offer to check your grammar for you, too. Because spelling is intertwined with grammar, do check. You always get to choose which grammar suggestions you take. Always. Think about how you want your words to sound on the page.

Most grammar checking tools will homogenize your author voice. I like short, somewhat choppy sentences. The grammar checkers want me to merge those sentences to smooth out the sentence. I don't.

Aside from assessing your spelling, watch for other kinds of word problems, such as acronyms, incorrect words or phrases, and capitalization.

Since I write for technical people and their management, I use TLAs (Three Letter Acronyms) a lot. Make sure that the first time you use an acronym of any length, you explain it, in parentheses, as I did. Then, make sure you use that acronym consistently. For example, a TLA is not the same as "tla." Your capitalization matters.

As for capitalization, only capitalize the proper nouns and the first word in a sentence. If you see you have other capitalizations, ask yourself if these capitals add to your reader's knowledge or entertainment.

Once you've checked your spelling and grammar, see how easy your writing is to read.

4.3.2 Check Your Readability

Most writing programs and grammar checkers include readability statistics. Some common readability statistics are:

- Flesch reading ease
- Flesch-Kincaid grade level
- Gunning-Fogg Index, which also reports a grade level.

Many word processing programs and editors have some form of built-in readability checker. You might have to search the menus for an entry that says "statistics" or "grammar checker."

I pay attention to the grade level and readability. Even though I write primarily for professionals, I try to keep my shorter writing at grade seven or below. Why should I make it difficult for my ideal reader to read what I have to say? For personal essays, I try to keep my writing at grade five or below.

To stay at that lower grade level, I look for passive voice, long sentences, and long paragraphs.

4.3.3 Decide When to Use Passive Voice

Grammar checkers always tell you when you have passive voice. Here's how to tell the difference:

- Active voice occurs when you see the subject first, and then the verb. An example: "I will miss him."
- Passive voice occurs when you can't tell who the subject is. "He will be missed."

In general, if you use the existential words, "is, be, are," you use passive voice. You always have the option to use passive voice. However, reread those sentences about missing someone.

With the active voice example, you know I will miss that person. But with the passive voice example, you can't tell. I claim he will be missed. By whom? Am I just making that up?

However, sometimes I purposefully use passive voice to show how people might feel as if they don't have autonomy. Here's an example:

> Then, the code arrives as if it was thrown over the wall.

Who threw the code over the wall? We can't tell, so it's passive voice. However, that served my purpose for that piece.

You're the writer. You always have the final say for long sentences and passive voice. Don't automatically take a grammar checker's suggestions. That said, the more passive voice you have, the more you challenge the reader. Readers might find it more challenging to read your writing.

Longer sentences also challenge readers.

4.3.4 Consider Shorter Sentences

You can also simplify your writing with shorter sentences. You've probably noticed I prefer short sentences. That's part of my author voice.

Here's an example sentence that might be too long at nineteen words:

> I use a guideline that says if your sentences regularly consist of twenty words or more, consider splitting them at the commas.

That's a 22-word sentence. I had to read it a couple of times, and I wrote it.

Here's an alternative of three shorter sentences, at a total of twenty-one words:

> Here's a guideline for sentence length. Are your sentences often twenty words or more? Consider splitting them where you see commas.

You always get to choose your sentence length. I happen to like shorter sentences. How will your ideal reader read your piece?

Our sentence length and paragraph structure reflect our author's voice. That said, I recommend you make shorter sentences and shorter paragraphs. Make it easy for your ideal reader to understand your words.

Can your reader read your words or do they feel intimidated by a wall of text?

4.3.5 Beware the Wall of Text

Part of readability is the length of the paragraphs themselves. The longer the paragraph, the more likely you have a wall of text.

As readers, our eyes glaze over when we encounter a wall of text. Who wants to try to read something that long? Worse, if you use long sentences *and* long paragraphs, your reader might quit reading.

 Where possible, write shorter paragraphs and add more subheadings to guide the reader.

For example, online readers tend to skim. Write shorter paragraphs and add subheadings to help people read your piece.

Here's how to visualize your paragraph length. Print your piece. Yes, on paper.

Let's assume you have roughly 1000 words in your piece. Depending on how you format it, that piece will be roughly two to four pages. In those 1000 words, you probably have three or four subheadings.

What does each page look like to you? Do you see a wall of text? If you see only one or two paragraphs, you might have a wall of text. If you have a page with several paragraphs and a subheading, you invite the reader in.

Shorter paragraphs—where they make sense—make it easier for your reader to comprehend your writing.

Now it's time to discuss language.

4.3.6 Simplify Your Language

Because you write from your expertise, you might use jargon, cleverness, or metaphors. You are familiar with those words. And, your ideal readers might love those words. However, you might alienate some readers you want to attract when you use those words and phrases.

> ### What if You Invent Words or Phrases?
>
> Maybe you invented a clever phrase, an acronym, or even a new word. Before you use any of these, ask yourself this question: What value do your inventions add to your reader's experience?
>
> If you think these inventions enhance the reader's experience, check yourself with The Rule of Three. Write down three reasons your inventions add to your reader's experience.
>
> If you can't find three reasons, reconsider your inventions. The more words or phrases you invent, the less accessible your writing is.

As a personal example, I've written articles about the Product Owner being an overloaded operator. The agile community will recognize the term "Product Owner." I've identified my ideal reader in the title of the article.

However, the overloaded operator phrase? That's a term from programming—not what these product owners do. I didn't stop with the title—I used the term in my article.

With jargon, I was too clever, and might have pushed *away* the very people I wanted to invite into my writing.

You might infer from the term that the person has too many roles and tasks. But I was not clear for my ideal reader, the product owner. Worse, once the product owner understood what I meant, that person might feel as if I condescended to them.

Instead, I could have used the title: "Product Owners: Overloaded and Underappreciated." The overloaded does include too many roles and too much work. And most people who are overloaded do feel as if they are underappreciated.

That gets the idea across without proving how clever I am. I want to make my reader feel smart.

You might have heard the writing expression, "Kill your darlings." Think of too much cleverness or jargon as candidate darlings. Do these terms invite your ideal readers into your writing? Do you show your ideal reader respect with these terms? Or, do you show your readers how smart you are?

 Make your *reader* feel smart.

If your writing does not invite or respect your ideal readers at any time, fix the words so you respect and speak the language of your readers.

Simplify your language wherever possible. Don't write down to readers, but make it easy for your readers to understand.

Part of that is how you use punctuation.

4.3.7 Choose Your Punctuation

What punctuation do you prefer to use?

I am the Queen—or the Empress—of the comma and the em-dash. I love them—mostly because they are versatile.

That said, I have at least two problems with my usage of commas and em-dashes:

- I tend to add commas when I take a sip of water or tea.
- Sometimes, I use an em-dash where I should use a period.

The more I use commas and em-dashes, the longer my sentence gets.

However, I write forward the way I want to. I don't "fix" my writing until I get to the editing part of the writing. I recommend you do that, too.

Punctuation, along with paragraphing, can help your reader speed through the piece—or it can slow them down, making them read carefully.

Choose based on the formality or informality of your writing and your author voice.

After you're all done writing, zoom out and look at a page of your writing. Consider these questions:

- Do you see punctuation marks that clutter the page?
- Is your capitalization consistent and correct?
- Do you italicize or bold "too many" words?

Writers might need to italicize some terms or phrases for emphasis. However, the more a writer uses italics, the less emphasis they create.

And if you want to bold some words, consider using a pull quote, such as this one:

 Bold helps people see the importance of one specific idea, such as this tip.

Writing an article is not the same as writing a text to your friend. You might use multiple question marks or exclamation points at the end of a sentence when you text. Use only one when you write for other people to read.

Now that you checked your technical correctness, review your logic.

4.4 Review Your Logic

Years ago, a colleague offered me this feedback on my writing. "I've seen people draw that kind of a conclusion with just two points. That's a little iffy. However, I've never seen anyone draw a conclusion with one piece of data."

That was his way of telling me I was missing some logic in that piece.

Back in Chapter 3, I suggested you consider three different structures. You can always verify your logic with those structures. However, you can also use an outline or a mind map to diagnose your piece.

4.4.1 Diagnose with an Outline or Mind Map

I've said all along that we think and learn as we write, which is why I hope you can postpone your outline or mind map until now. I've suggested that settling on a conclusion too early shortcuts your thinking and learning.

However, if you worry about your logic, consider using an outline or a mind map as a diagnostic tool.

Outline your piece as you wrote it. Or create a mind map from the piece.

Does your outline or mind map make sense? Is it missing anything? Does it have more ideas than you thought you wanted to write?

If you are missing something, return to cycling and write forward. If you have too many ideas, remove them from the piece and add them back to your fieldstones.

You can also ask for feedback, which I'll address in Chapter 5. However, I learn more when I diagnose my writing first. You might, too.

You're happy now with the structure, but your piece is too long. You need to reduce the length.

4.4.2 Reduce Length

You finished your writing and your piece is too long. You're supposed to write a 1000-word article, but it's 1500 words. What can you do?

You already checked, and it's one solid article, not two ideas masquerading as one article. You need to cut words. (If you do have several ideas, remove those extra ideas and put them back into your fieldstones. Then, review your subheadings and transitions and wrap the article.)

Use the Rule of Three as an idea. Cut a third of the: words, sentences, or paragraphs. (Yes, I first learned this from *Weinberg on Writing* WOW14. Weinberg suggests experimenting with any fraction from 1/3 to 1/10. In my experience, 1/3 works well for many of my writing colleagues and for me.

Consider this from the word out to the sentence out to the paragraph. First, cut a third of the words in every sentence. Then, cut a third of the sentences in each paragraph. Then, cut a third of the paragraphs.

Or, start from the paragraph down to the word: First cut a third of the paragraphs. Then, a third of the sentences. Then a third of the words.

Here are some possibilities to see what to cut:

- Simplify your sentences. You might have repeated information in various ways. When you simplify your sentences, you see the repetition.

- Add in necessary details. Sometimes, writers try to reduce their word count by removing details. Add those details back in and then review this article's structure. You might have two articles (or more). Once you see everything you learned by writing, you can decide how to restructure the piece.
- Leave this piece alone. Write a new one. This piece might be precisely the right length for the ideas you want to express. Instead of trying to cut words, reduce the *ideas* in the article and write a new one.

Now that you've edited and checked the structure, make sure you maintain your author voice.

4.5 Maintain Your Author Voice

Always correct your spelling. However, all the other advice I offered in this chapter? You decide whether to take it or leave it.

Consider reading your writing out loud to see if you like what's on the page. When I say out loud, I mean that if someone walked by, they would hear you talk. Do not say words in your head. Use your mouth so you can hear the words in your ears. Then, if you do like the piece, stop editing and publish.

Alternatively, use the text-to-speech capability on your computer or in your browser to read the piece to you. You will hear what's wrong or awkward phrasing.

Your job as a writer is to discover how you sound on the page. Then, practice writing more pieces to reinforce what you like and diminish what you don't like.

That writing practice means it's more important for you to write and publish a piece than it is to "perfect" a single piece of writing.

4.6 Add References

As a nonfiction writer, sooner or later you'll reference other people's words.

Always create some kind of a reference when you refer to books, articles, and any idea that isn't common knowledge.

For example, while we all know prediction is tricky, if I want to refer to Yogi Berra's quote, I would cite it like this:

> "It's tough to make predictions, especially about the future." —Yogi Berra

If you reference an online article in an online article, you might just be able to link to that source. However, if you reference a book, you need to cite that book. (The book does not have to be in print to cite it. Any book, regardless of format, needs a citation.)

You've noticed I've referenced several books and articles in this book so far. I've created bibliographic references for the books, and links for the online articles.

> ### Keep Notes on Research References
>
> Especially if you write for a formal journal, track your research references. Note the author, title, source, and page number.
>
> If you use a lot of research in your writing, use an application or database, so you can always find the reference.

Even though I've used an informal tone in this book, I did not use informal references. I use APA style references. There are other styles. If you write for academic journals, learn the style they prefer and use that.

Even with proper attribution, writers have limitations on how much they can quote. For example, never quote song lyrics. Because songs are so short, you can almost never quote from a song without violating the songwriter's copyright. (See Chapter 6 for a *brief* discussion of copyright.)

And if you have several quotations from one source, consider paraphrasing those words instead of including all those words.

In general, use your words, not someone else's words. Refer to other people's work, but don't copy. Copying is a form of plagiarism. Don't do it.

Now that you're totally, finally done with your piece, finish your title.

4.7 Finalize Your Title

Back in Chapter 2, I suggested you focus your writing with a title. Now, it's time to create a title that draws your ideal reader into your writing.

Nonfiction titles are a little different than the rest of your writing. Your title needs to identify your ideal reader and why that person should read your piece. Titles attract and influence your readers to read more.

That means nonfiction titles are a form of copywriting. For article or blog post titles, consider reading "How to Write Magnetic Headlines[1]."

Copywriting attracts your ideal reader. Copywriting is a form of influence, of marketing. Especially if you write online, you'll need a title that draws your ideal reader into your piece.

---

[1] https://copyblogger.com/magnetic-headlines/

Back in Chapter 2, I said I would use this title to focus my writing: "Use stories to explain status." That's a bad title because it doesn't invite my ideal reader, the project manager, into the piece.

Good titles invite your ideal reader into your piece.

Start with the problem and the benefits for your title:

- Use the problem as part of the title. For example, "Avoid Boring Status Reports: Tell Stories Instead."
- "How to" and add what people want. "How to Engage Leaders in Project Status."
- A number of "Secrets" or Tips and add the problem. "Three Secrets to Engage Leaders in Project Status Reports."

Sometimes, you might use risks or surprise:

- A number of "Common Mistakes". "Three Common Mistakes of Traditional Project Status Reports."
- Power words that evoke emotion, such as living or dying. "Avoid Death by PowerPoint and Engage Leaders with Project Stories.
- Surprise or focus: "Stories About Users: A Surprising Option for Project Status Reports.

You might like some of these. Since I have trouble titling my articles, I test my titles with headline analyzers.

I use two analyzers to test my titles: Coschedule.com[2] and AMI, Advanced Marketing Institute[3]. They often give contradictory results, so you might decide to choose between them, not choose a title that works equally well.

Here are the results from the titles above:

---
[2] https://coschedule.com/headline-analyzer
[3] https://www.aminstitute.com/

1. Avoid Boring Status Reports: Tell Stories Instead. Not great on either analyzer.
2. How to Engage Leaders in Project Status. Not great on Coschedule, but stellar on AMI.
3. Three Secrets to Engage Leaders in Project Status Reports. Great on Coschedule, Good on AMI.
4. Three Common Mistakes of Traditional Project Status Reports. Okay on Coschedule and Good on AMI.
5. Avoid Death by PowerPoint and Engage Leaders with Project Stories. So-so on both.
6. Stories About Users: A Surprising Option for Project Status Reports. Okay on Coschedule, Good on AMI.

If I don't like any of these, I might reread the article from the top and see if a title jumps out at me. But, since this is an article and not a book title, I would stop here. I'll take one of the good titles and be done with it.

When in doubt, choose a title that describes your piece, not a title with good copywriting numbers. Write for people, not for algorithms. That's because your readers know where to find you. While you might want more readers, algorithms tend to attract people who might not be your ideal readers.

4.8 Practice Editing Just Enough

Now it's time for you to practice editing. Take the piece you completed at the end of Chapter 3 and edit it. How little can you edit?

1. Check all your spelling. Verify your grammar is what you want.
2. What readability score do you have? Are you satisfied with that readability? If not, make a copy of your piece and

try some alternatives, such as removing passive voice and shortening your sentences or paragraphs. Compare the two copies when you're finished and decide which version you prefer. You're in charge of your writing.
3. Finalize your title.

We can't know what perfection is, so don't bother trying to create perfection. Instead, finish editing so readers can read. Then publish this piece and write the next piece.

Now, we'll go on to when you ask people for feedback or review.

5. Choose the Feedback You Want

You get to choose when and how to ask for feedback on any piece of writing.

You might want other people to offer you feedback on your writing. You have these choices: open feedback, editor-based feedback, and peer review.

If you write for academic journals, "peer review" often means an anonymous, specific form of peer review. I'm not going to discuss that here. When I say peer review, I mean "review from people you consider your peers."

The more you write for other people, the more likely you will encounter a professional editor. And if you want to build a local writing community, you can ask for and receive peer review.

Let's start with why you want feedback.

5.1 What Will Feedback Offer You?

Some writers want to "know" if their writing is any good. They want validation.

Remember, no writing can ever be perfect. That means you can't "know" your writing is good. Instead, use the ideas in this book to learn as you write, and publish.

The more you write and publish, the more you will learn how to write.

If you want validation, publish pieces more often. Don't bother with specific feedback. Instead, go meta, and ask yourself, "Do people know me for my writing yet?" If not, write and publish more.

That said, I have asked for feedback on my unpublished blog posts twice—out of 3000 blog posts. Both times when I was concerned I got facts wrong and I'd already checked the facts.

Before you ask someone else for feedback, consider how you will be ready for feedback. In Chapter 4, I suggested you read out loud or have the computer read your piece to you. The listening and writing parts of our brain are different, and you might gain a new perspective or insight about your writing.

Before you ask for feedback, there's still one more piece to know about feedback. Wait until you're all done to ask for feedback.

5.2 Never Ask for Interim Feedback

If you speak with other writers, you'll hear all about interim feedback. Do writers need interim feedback?

No. Absolutely not. Do not ask for interim feedback and if someone asks you for interim feedback on their writing, decline.

Why?

Because nonfiction writing integrates thinking and learning. The more often you stop for feedback, the more you stop yourself. You stop thinking and learning and you have more work in progress. Both states are deadly for nonfiction writers.

What if you want feedback on the ideas?

Reframe that question to this one: How can your reader offer you feedback when you're not done thinking?

I used the analogy of writing nonfiction to writing code back in Chapter 1. Maybe that analogy didn't work for you. Instead, consider the analogy of cooking a fudgy chocolate cake. (If you don't like chocolate, choose a recipe where you separate the mixing of the ingredients in some way.)

The first step in that recipe is to melt very dark chocolate with the fat. If I asked someone to taste that mixture, it would be bitter. No one would want to eat that part of the cake. That's because there's no sugar.

The second step is to mix the eggs and the sugar. If someone tasted that part, it would be way too sweet. Even sweet-lovers would not want a cake with only that mixture.

Until I mix both parts together, no taster can see what the cake might taste like. Even then, the cake tastes different when it's cooked. The raw batter does not taste like the cooked batter.

Think of your ideas as the bitter chocolate mixture. Then, think of your stories, anecdotes, and examples as the sweet egg mixture.

Getting feedback on just one part of the recipe doesn't work. You need feedback on the entire cooked recipe—after you finish the baking.

That's why getting early feedback on the ideas doesn't work for writers.

If you worry that some of your ideas "don't work," finish writing *first*. Include all the examples and your words, using the ideas in Chapters 3 and 4.

There are some times when feedback makes sense.

5.3 When Feedback Makes Sense

These are circumstances when feedback might make sense for you:

- You're building a writing community, possibly at work, and you want to be able to support each other.

- You're relatively new to writing and you're writing something other than a blog post, such as a magazine or journal article.
- You're submitting an article that you expect will undergo additional peer review or editing and you want to make sure the article is clear and as clean as possible before you submit it.

In general, beware of writing communities who "review"—or more likely—critique or criticize your work. Those communities tend to be new writers who don't know how to write or offer feedback—or both.

A critique is supposed to be a critical examination of the work. Often, that's what readers did when they examined a book or other writing. However, most people equate critique with criticism. Too often, criticism takes direct aim at a writer's self-esteem. That doesn't help a writer get better.

If these people don't know how to write or offer feedback, don't ask them for feedback. Instead, write, edit as little as possible, and publish as often as possible. Allow comments wherever you publish that piece. You'll learn from your writing and publishing practice. In addition, you'll learn from reader comments. That's because those readers are your ideal readers.

However, you might want to build relationships with peers where you can offer each other feedback. You might offer feedback about the ideas in your pieces and your writing.

This kind of feedback has a name: "peer review."

5.4 Clarify the Value of Peer Review

Peers share a context with you. That context might include your company, job, or expertise. Since they share that context, they might offer valuable feedback.

When reviewers comment on your work, they might offer useful feedback. However, if reviewers change your words, they act as editors.

You might find peer review, in the form of comments, helpful. I find comments quite helpful from my reviewers. I rarely find their word changes helpful.

If you want a more formal peer review framework, take a look at the software patterns community. They've run patterns conferences since 1993 and have a specific framework for offering comments as feedback[1].

Because peer review offers comments, you always have the choice to integrate or address those comments.

If you prefer not to use the peer feedback framework from the patterns community, ask for feedback about clarity, organization, and possibly, the ideas.

One way to do that is to use the Perfection Game.

5.5 Consider the Perfection Game

Some product development teams use a retrospective activity called "The Perfection Game[2]." To adapt the game for writing feedback, do this:

1. Ask a reviewer to play the Perfection Game with you. Once they agree, send them your writing.
2. The reviewer rates the value of the writing on a scale of 1 to 10, where 10 is totally valuable and the reviewer doesn't see any way to improve it.
3. The reviewer explains, "Here's what I liked about this writing," and lists what they liked.

---

[1] https://www.hillside.net/documents/PatternLanguageForWritersWorkshops.pdf
[2] https://thecoreprotocols.org/protocols/perfectiongame.html

4. Then the reviewer offers improvements in the form, "To make it a 10 for me, you would have to do X." X is the list of what the reviewer sees as improvements.

The Perfection Game works very well for peers, people who share the same context.

I've reviewed conference proposals where we played the Perfection Game. That worked quite well.

When your peers are not your ideal reader, the game might not work that well.

If you and your readers share a context, consider teaching your readers the Perfection Game. If they like the game, they might use it.

However, you might want to learn how to offer feedback and see how a writer receives your feedback first.

In my experience, few writers know how to ask for feedback. I recommend not more than three questions for feedback.

5.6 Use These Questions for Feedback

What do you need to know when you ask for feedback? Based on the Rule of Three from Chapter 3, consider these questions:

- Did I lose you anywhere?
- Am I missing anything?
- Do I need an image somewhere?

Those questions are about how the piece connects with the ideal reader, including clarity and logic.

If in doubt, ask fewer questions of any reviewer. You can use the "Did I lose you anywhere question" alone and often get great feedback.

The more questions you ask, the reviewer expects to find something "bad." They focus on the questions, not the piece you gave them to read.

If you want feedback, you might need to offer it. Use empathy when you offer feedback.

5.7 Offer Feedback with Empathy

By now, we know writers think and learn as they write. That means the manuscript might not precisely reflect what that writer wanted to say. That's why I recommend you never critique or criticize a manuscript.

Instead, use empathy to offer information or comments about the clarity and organization of the writing.

Explain your reaction to what you read.

For example, a colleague, George Dinwiddie, offered me terrific feedback when he reviewed one of my books. His comment was: "I'm tired of you telling me 'You need to do' this or that thing."

I searched for "You need to" and found way too many instances of that phrase. I now use the word "Consider this" or "Consider these options." Those words respect my reader much more than my previous words.

I learn a ton from my reviewers when they say:

- "What did you mean here?" Or "Did you mean?" Or "I don't understand this part."
- "I lost track halfway through this sentence."
- "I needed this information earlier."

Each of these questions helps writers see where they might need to clarify the topic, the logic, or the structure.

That's useful feedback. Writers can see what confused their readers. The writer has hints about what to fix.

 Always offer feedback so the writer sees where you stopped understanding.

What if you loved the piece? Try something like this: "I understood all of it. Thanks for letting me read it. Where will you publish it?"

What if you don't like the writer's style of writing? You can say, "I'm not your ideal reader."

You don't have to say anything else. Don't apologize or try to make it up to the writer. Just say, "I'm not your ideal reader."

However, some feedback doesn't serve the writer. It only serves the reviewer.

5.8 Beware of Reviewer-Focused Feedback

Reviewer-focused feedback is any form of evaluation, including praise.

Praise, such as, "I liked it" is lovely, and is a form of validation. However, if I don't know *why* the person liked it, the feedback doesn't offer value to me.

If you receive praise, consider asking about specifics: what they learned or enjoyed. I've also received criticism:

- "You're wrong."
- "Terrible."

- "I would give this a C- if I was grading this article."

When I receive criticism, I often discover the reviewer and I do *not* share the same context. That person is not my peer, and often not my ideal reader. If I want to reach those people, I would need to write a different piece.

Now that you know how to offer peer feedback, consider if you want to build a review community.

5.9 Build Your Peer Community

Now that you know how to offer and receive writing feedback, you might want to build your peer review community. I've seen this work quite well inside organizations and with colleagues who are a peer group.

I've used my peer group to learn how my peers react to:

- Images, especially if those images are in progress.
- How I organized a specific piece of several pieces.
- The pros and cons of various publishing sites.

Early in my writing career, I asked other experts in my field for feedback. They knew how to offer feedback. They were gracious enough to do so, and I returned the favor when they asked.

Since more people read than write, you might find it relatively easy to find reviewers, especially if you explain how you would like them to offer you feedback.

In addition, some nonfiction writers work together. I'm most familiar with consultants who want to help each other improve. In that case, consider how you might create a writing community.

5.10 Create a Writing Community

If you want a writing community, define its purpose and your working agreements. Your community might offer more than just feedback on your writing.

Consider these purposes:

- Discover and share publishing options and opportunities.
- Discuss the business of writing and publishing.
- How to evolve your system of writing and publishing, including accountability.

Only you know why you want a writing community.

Working agreements explain how you will treat each other and the kinds of topics you will and will not discuss. For example, several of my writing communities agree to never discuss politics or religion. Some communities offer support and others work more as masterminds.

Define the purpose first. Then create your community.

5.11 Practice Your Feedback Choices

Consider these options for writing feedback:

1. When do you *know* you don't need writing feedback? When can you publish without feedback?
2. What will trigger your request for feedback?
3. How will you request feedback? How will you train your reviewers to give you useful feedback?
4. Do you have a peer review community? If you want that community, how will you invite people into that community?

Now that you know about feedback, let's discuss your publishing options and how to work with editors.

6. Publish Your Work

Before you can publish, you need to know who owns your writing. You might own your writing. You might write for someone else, such as your employer.

Once you know who owns your writing, you can choose how and where to publish.

6.1 You Own Your Writing

In general, assuming you write alone, you own the copyright to your writing. You don't even have to write "© Your Name" on the piece. Unless you sign an agreement that gives your copyright to someone else, you own your words.

However, you might have signed an agreement that gives your copyright to your employer. Most people sign an NDA, Non-Disclosure Agreement, to work at a company. Sometimes that NDA contains a non-compete agreement.

Regardless of what you signed, your company might have added a section that says they own all your writing. Not just what you write at work, but all your words including fiction and other nonfiction. They think your writing might compete with their products.

If you're not sure, check your NDA. If you don't have a copy of your NDA, ask for it. Regardless of what you signed before, you can ask to renegotiate that agreement now.

Even if you have the ability to write outside of work, never write or publish anything internal or confidential. Don't write something that anyone could link back to any part of your work because that would violate your NDA. Instead, *fictionalize* everything you see at work.

 Never embarrass people with your publication, including yourself. Fictionalize your work to write about other people's challenges.

Let's assume you own your words. Read Fishman's *The Copyright Handbook: What Every Writer Needs to Know* FIS17 to learn all about copyright. You might want to review the section in Chapter 4 about referencing other people and their material.

What if you co-write with another writer? *Before* you start any discussions or writing, ask that person to check their NDA to make sure they own their words. And, clarify how you both will use your words together. I recommend you create a contract with everything specified, especially in the event of one author's death. In the US, copyright extends to 70 years past the author's death.

That's the very short explanation of when you own your copyright and your writing.

Depending on the contract you signed when you started to work, your company might own your writing.

6.2 Your Employer Owns Your Writing

If writing is part of your responsibilities, your employer owns any writing you do for work. Do check your NDA and non-compete to make sure your company doesn't own all your words, regardless of whether you write for their business interests.

Here are examples where your company might own the words you write for them, but not the words you write for yourself:

- You work for a consulting company. The company owns any reports you write for clients. However, you can write your own blogs or articles.
- You're a technical writer, but they don't care if you write nonfiction or fiction outside of work.
- When you're a contractor, the company might own your code or other deliverables. However, they don't own your other writing.

If you want to write nonfiction separate from your employer's interests, negotiate a new NDA or non-compete before you start writing. The company has lawyers on retainer who can make your life miserable.

One more caution: If you work for an employer, never, ever use any of your employer's technology to write. As soon as you do, your employer might think they have the rights to your words. I'm not a lawyer, so don't construe this as legal advice.

Especially if you own your words, you might choose to write for hire. Sometimes, your employer might encourage you to write for hire, too, because of your ideal readers.

6.3 Write as Work for Hire

As you build your writing reputation, some websites, magazines, or journals might ask you to write for them. Sometimes, those publishers want to own your copyright. Your writing then becomes a work for hire.

You sign an agreement (often in exchange for money) with the publisher. As soon as you sign that agreement, and deliver your piece to them, they own your copyright to that specific piece.

When should you write for other publishers? It depends on how well they will help you reach your ideal readers and cement your reputation. How will that publication enhance your career?

Here are some considerations for deciding when to write for other publications:

- What is the readership of that publication? You can ask for information about the kind of readers and how many readers that publication has.
- Does the publication request your copyright? If so, what do you get in return for that copyright? Every contract is a negotiation.

You might negotiate these items:

- A reasonable fee to write the piece.
- A bio with a link back to your site or some social media site.
- An agreement on when you can republish this piece on your site, with an acknowledgment that the publisher owns the copyright.

In addition, consider these possible contract terms:

- What happens if the publisher ceases publishing, especially online?
- What formats does the publisher want to publish in? The publisher might only want electronic rights. Do you have print, audio, or translation rights?

There's nothing wrong with writing as work for hire. As long as you know that's what your writing is. I still write regular columns for one site, because their readers are my ideal readers and they have a huge readership.

6.4 Write for Publishers Who Don't Want Your Copyright

I've worked with publishers who only wanted first electronic publication rights. First publication rights means this publisher has *exclusive* right to your content for the duration of those rights. In my experience, those rights tend to be 30 or 60 days.

Always negotiate a contract with these publishers, too. Review the items to negotiate as in the previous section. Since they don't want your copyright, these publishers tend to pay less than the publishers who want your copyright.

Remember, when the publisher does not want your copyright, you own that piece in all forms, after the first publication rights period is over. You can republish the piece on your site.

I enjoyed writing for magazines for years. Early in my career, I learned a lot from their professional editors.

6.5 How to Work with a Professional Editor

Professional editors can help you become a better writer.

Do not use a professional editor if you're writing for your blog or other relatively short and informal writing. Write, check your spelling and grammar, and then publish your piece. Continue to write and publish. You'll learn much more from writing and publishing practice than if you hire an editor.

Sometimes, magazines or journals will have you work with two different people: a technical editor and a professional copyeditor.

A technical editor helps you shape your article. In my experience, technical editors often have expertise in the field, in addition to their writing experience. However, they rarely are professional editors. When technical editors do their job right, they will offer suggestions for clarity and organization.

Copyeditors focus more on grammar, wording, and how the piece looks on the page.

These two editors have just one job: help the writers sound more like themselves, but clearer. They are supposed to help you, the writer, retain your author voice, while clarifying your words and ideas.

Not all technical editors and copyeditors understand their roles. I've worked with too many technical editors who wanted to write my article the way they would. And, I've worked with professional copyeditors who wanted to remove my author voice—to make my article sound generic, just like everyone else's.

You don't have to take their suggestions.

You are the writer. Choose which editing suggestions to take and which to reject. If either editor gave you a "final" article you're supposed to rubber-stamp, don't just accept it. Instead, ask the editor to track their changes so they don't change your words directly. Now, you can see what they thought would make your piece clearer. You can decide which changes you will take.

If the magazine has significant editorial preferences, they might offer you a style sheet in advance. Use that information to decide if you want to write for that outlet.

Now that you've seen other options, let's focus on your personal publication options.

6.6 Choose Your Publication Options

Many of my writing colleagues want to write to build their reputations as knowledgeable experts. That means they want to publish somewhere their ideal readers can find them.

Consider these options for where to place your writing:

- Your own site first, so your readers always know where to find you. Then, share that link on social media.
- A newsletter to connect with and reinforce your subscribers.
- Other sites or magazines. In your bio, include a link back to your site.

Let's start with your site.

6.6.1 Publish on Your Site

If you want to build a brand, publish your writing on your site first. Create a blog and regularly write posts there. And if you write a newsletter, make sure you post those back issues on your site.

When I say "your site," I mean a site that has your name somehow associated with the site.

Several large blogging platforms allow you to start a blog for free. Research or ask colleagues what they use for a blogging platform.

If you have a site with your name associated with it, you have many choices about how to present your writing to your readers. You can often include a link to a newsletter signup. If you don't have your own space on the web, you don't have that option.

I've seen collective blogs with several writers, especially those who are a part of a collaborative consulting practice. Do publish there, especially if your posts include your name and a link to your bio.

The more you write and publish, the more you create and reinforce your brand. Can you write a monthly newsletter and a daily blog? If you can't blog daily, how often can you write every week? The more often you write and publish, the faster you will build your brand. And, the better your writing will become.

Build a writing and publishing cadence, so your readers know what to expect. And you'll build your brand faster.

Branding is a long-term game. The more writing you have associated with your name, the more likely your content will show up in searches. The more likely your ideal readers will read your content.

Without a critical mass of content, very few people can find you. You won't find it easy to discern or build your brand. The more you write, the more you can refine your brand. Use an incremental approach to writing and publishing.

The more you write and publish, the faster you build your brand. And you'll probably realize you have more ideas about what to write. The more I write, the more ideas I have for my idea bank.

Don't worry about your readership. Even if you write daily, your readership will vary with what's going on in your area of expertise and the world.

Keep writing and publishing. The more you write and publish the better the chance your readers will find you.

After you publish on your site, use social media to publicize your writing. Include a link back to your site when you use social media. As I write this, social media appears to give preference to posts with images. While that might change, images that attract readers might help your publicity efforts.

Some writers I know publish on a general publication site, such as Medium. I don't recommend you *start* writing on Medium because they don't build your brand. They publicize their publishing. That's their business model.

All the other social media sites work the same way. They want your content to build their reputation as a publisher.

You can still use any social site. Write on your site first, and republish on the social site. Always include a link back to your original post.

6.6.2 Publish a Newsletter

Newsletters help build your brand. You choose what to write and at which frequency. You can build your brand and fan base, one newsletter at a time.

When you publish a newsletter, never use your personal email to send newsletters. Always use a company whose sole purpose is to send emails. You can use services such as Substack for free if you don't charge your readers. Or, you might consider a mailing list provider, such as ConvertKit.

Regardless of the newsletter service you use, always include a link back to your site where your readers can read more of what you write.

6.7 Recognize When Others Violate Your Copyright

I use images in many of my books, blog posts, and articles. Whenever I see my images on other people's articles, I see that other people violated my copyright.

If I see a presentation with my images, I email them and explain that they violated my copyright. I normally ask these people to redo their presentation, acknowledging that all the images are mine, and that they have permission to use those images. In addition, I ask them to point back to my book and my site.

However, people don't just copy images. Sometimes, they copy entire blog posts, articles, or chapters of books. If they post the information online, I first write a firm and clear email and ask them to remove my material from their site. If that doesn't work, writers can issue a take-down notice to their ISP (Internet Service Provider). Often, the ISP will remove the site.

So far, most of the time, these are people who claim not to know about copyright.

However, some people don't appear to care. They persist with their theft of your property.

Now it's time for you to decide. Does this person have enough of a following that you will suffer harm from their theft? If no, I often ignore them. It's not worth spending emotional time on them.

However, sometimes, the thieves need to know their actions affected me. That's when it's time for a lawyer. So far, I've only had to invest enough money for a lawyer to write a letter. The thieves finally chose to take down their plagiarizing work.

Learn about copyright with *The Copyright Handbook: What Every Writer Needs to Know* FIS17. And decide when you would act to protect your copyright.

6.8 Publish Widely

If you want to become well-known, build your publication network to publish widely.

Do write for the people who already know about you. And, expand your publishing horizons when you write for and publish on another site, such as a magazine or a professional journal.

You get to decide which other outlets you write for and when. The more you publish, the more chances your ideal reader has to find you.

The more I wrote for other outlets, the more ideal readers I could attract back to my site. Since I had plenty more content for these readers, they signed up for my newsletter.

Those people think of me as a knowledgeable expert. These readers want to read my writing because it educates, influences, and sometimes, entertains them.

How much do you want to write and publish? You might need to build up to whatever pace works for you.

The more you write and publish, the better your writing will be. And the more people will find you.

6.9 Practice Publishing Your Work

Consider these ideas for publishing your writing:

1. Determine if you own the copyright to all your words. If not, who do you need to speak with, to see what you can do for your personal writing?
2. Consider how much time you want to devote to writing and publishing. Write down how many blog posts, articles, and newsletters you want to write each month.
3. What changes might you need to make with your schedule to commit to that writing and publishing?
4. Where will you primarily publish? What other outlets will you consider, under which circumstances?

Now that you understand all the writing and publishing aspects, consider the tips in the following chapter.

7. Help Yourself Succeed

As you practice writing, how can you help yourself succeed to become a better writer? I've offered you many suggestions about how to write. However, you might discover that you need something a little different.

How you implement those ideas? That's up to you.

To write easily, create a writing environment that works for you.

7.1 Create Your Writing Environment

Throughout this book, I've said to write and cycle, edit, and then publish. That means writers need to reduce all the friction in their writing. Start with your environment to reduce friction, both physically and mentally. Let's start with the physical.

I hope you tried the various freewriting practice sessions. Reflect back on any of those sessions. How did you physically feel when you practiced freewriting? If you were not physically comfortable, here's a checklist that might work for you as you write on a computer:

1. Your feet are flat on the floor, not dangling in the air.
2. Your chair supports your arms.
3. Your wrists are flat, not cocked up or down.
4. Your keyboard doesn't require too much pressure and helps you maintain good wrist and hand positions. (I don't use my laptop keyboard. Instead, I use a separate ergonomic keyboard.)

In addition, I use large monitors, so I don't have to squint to see the screen.

If you prefer to write longhand, choose a pen that glides across the paper easily. I like inexpensive gel pens. You might prefer a different pen. As long as the pen glides, your pen will work.

I also reduce mental friction with this checklist:

1. Turn off all notifications. Since I don't want interruptions, I turn off all machine and cell notifications. I also leave my phone on silent mode. That way, I can focus on my writing, including my thinking and learning.
2. Only listen to music without words. If I listen to music with words, I start to type those words.
3. Keep water or tea close at hand, for hydration.
4. Get up and walk around every so often.

While writing does not use many calories—much to my dismay—it uses brainpower. Humans need water or other hydrating fluids to maintain that brainpower.

Throughout this book, I've suggested you work in 15-minute timeboxes, with possible planning and reflection as you proceed. That timing is quite similar to the Pomodoro Technique.

In a Pomodoro, you work for 25 minutes and then take a five-minute break to stand, move, and stretch. After your break, you repeat the 25-minute working session. (See *Pomodoro Technique Illustrated: The Easy Way to Do More in Less Time* NOT10 for more details.)

I walk in my breaks, especially if I'm unsure how to write the next chunk. Even if I'm temporarily stuck, just a couple of minutes into my walk, I realize what the next chunk is.

My checklists help me reduce all the physical and mental friction that allows me to write fast and well. The ideas behind the checklists help me write more words.

You might like to gamify your word count as I do.

7.2 Count Your Words

I track how many words I write every day. I maintain a spreadsheet so I can track my writing progress. You might consider that, too, especially if you want to write and publish a lot.

My spreadsheet works because I compete with myself. The number of words is just a number. However, the existence of that number on a daily, weekly, or monthly basis proves to *me* how much I start and finish. I use these guidelines for how I count my words:

- As I write books, I count the words I wrote. That way, I can see daily progress.
- I don't count words in blog posts and newsletters until I publish them. That reinforces my need to publish more often.

My word counts help me create and reinforce two types of streaks. The first streak is the number of days or weeks I write in a row. While I might not be able to write every single day, I can often write each week.

The second streak is the number of words I write daily or weekly. Since I count book words as I write them, I can see if I'm waffling on finishing a given book in my spreadsheet.

My word counts and how they appear in my spreadsheet offer me reinforcing feedback. The more days I write and the more words I write, the better my spreadsheet "looks." All those boxes have numbers in them.

Since I compete with myself, the content of the spreadsheet matters to me. You might not find these ideas of word counts or writing streaks helpful. However, I do recommend you count your words.

You'll see how your 15-minute sessions help you finish your writing.

I don't count words in my idea bank or fieldstones. That's because all those words end up in something I publish.

Some writers I know also track the time it takes to write their words. I have yet to succeed at tracking time. If you learn to track your time, let me know how you do it.

One way to get more words is to avoid *talking* about your writing instead of writing.

7.3 Avoid Talking About Your Writing

Writers who talk about their writing don't always finish what they say they're working on. As a big-time extrovert, I rarely discuss any in-progress writing. I never discuss blog posts or articles in progress. I finish and publish them.

I rarely discuss books in progress, until I'm ready to ask for technical review.

That's because extroverts, especially, can talk away their books. Once we tell people about it, why bother writing it? The information is out there. In the air, but it's out there.

Except, readers can't consume that airborne information.

Write the book, post, or article. Don't talk about writing it.

If you are also an extrovert, consider this approach instead of telling people you're writing anything, especially a book:

- Write a series of blog posts or articles about this particular topic.

- Give a conference talk about some aspect of the topic. Consider your ideal readers and what they want to know.
- As part of your presentation, ask the audience for their questions. Take those questions to write more about the topic.

Once you have "enough" blog posts, articles, and presentations, then, write the book. You might learn, as I have, that the shorter pieces help me decide what's in or out of this possible book.

Twenty-five years ago, a colleague, Dan, told me he was writing a book with a Big Name in the field. Dan has not written anything about that topic in any form. No blog posts, no articles, and definitely no book. However, Dan talked his book away every time we saw each other professionally.

That's books. What about a particular blog post? Instead of discussing it, consider writing something "incomplete." Write as much of the post as you can. Add a line at the bottom and ask people what questions they have. Then, publish and see how people respond.

You might be done with this piece and not realize it.

When you read widely, you might see more options for how to write.

7.4 Read Widely

I never planned to write at all. When I started my consulting business, I wrote to market myself.

However, I read everything from the time I could read cereal boxes. I read through school and early adulthood. Later, as with most parents of small children, I had years when I barely read a book every month or two. However, children don't stay small forever, and I returned to reading.

How often and what can you read? Read everything: newspapers, magazines, shorter online words. Read nonfiction and fiction. The more you read, the more you will absorb how other writers write.

You might think you need to read with purpose. Instead, read for information and enjoyment first. Let that writer educate, influence, and entertain you. Then, when you finish reading, ask yourself about the value and enjoyment you received from that piece of writing.

What did the writer do? Did the writer use the structures I recommend in Chapter 3, to start with a problem and make the piece interesting? Maybe that writer did something totally different that appeals to you more?

Note what the writer did. If you enjoyed the information and the reading experience, consider studying that piece for what worked and didn't work for *you* as a reader.

For example, in my field, several nonfiction books incorporate stories. If you got this far, you know I like stories, too. However, I'm so frustrated with some of those writers that I refuse to discuss my reactions in public. Their books don't work for *me* and frustrate me no end.

As a reader, I had to work too hard to enjoy the books. I had to make the connections that images or summaries would have provided me.

I learned from what I didn't like as much as what I liked about those books.

What if you don't like some piece of writing? It might not be to your taste. The writer's voice might not appeal to you. Or, you don't believe the writer. You don't have to finish reading everything you start. Instead, read something new. Although, you might want to consider spending five minutes deciding *why* that piece didn't appeal to you.

If nothing appeals to you, ask yourself if you're criticizing other people's writing. Instead, find something you're sure you'll enjoy and read that.

Remember to read fiction, also. Any kind of genre fiction, because you'll absorb the structure. And you'll see how different writers draw readers in.

One caveat for fiction: I don't read any literary fiction with big honking paragraphs and highfaluting, pompous language. For me, most literary fiction is too difficult to read. I read genre fiction. I enjoy reading it, and it informs all my writing.

The more widely you read, the more you can see options for how you can improve your writing. You might want to write, collaborating with other people.

7.5 Write With Others

One way to change your writing system is to experiment writing with other people. Some writers call this "cowriting."

Every pair will find their own way—or stop cowriting. I've used several approaches, depending on whether I sit with the other writer in real-time, work at distance in real-time, or work asynchronously.

In all cases, the two of us first discuss the topic. Then, if we work in real-time, we approach the writing as if we're pair-programming.

If we sit together, we literally exchange the physical keyboard every few minutes. I recommend you agree in advance on how often you will exchange the keyboard.

If we write at distance, we use a collaborative tool, such as google docs. Not only do we agree on how frequently we change who will write forward, but we also need an agreement about when we can fix typos behind the writer who's writing forward. I've had several successful collaborations when we pair-write and agree on how we will write forward and fix typos.

I've also used asynchronous writing, where we agreed on the topic, and then decided how much one of us would write before sending the document to the other person. I call this "ping-pong," where the document goes back and forth between the two writers. Since our real-time collaboration tools are so good now, I haven't used this approach for a decade or more.

Before you start to write together, agree on how you will manage the intellectual property the two of you create. And if you're thinking of writing a book, start with an article—or two. That shorter writing is a test of your ability to write together.

Since every writer is different, you'll encounter writers who want to interrupt themselves with editing. Or who want to put the piece away for a week or more. Or who doesn't like the anecdotes and examples that you do.

Twice, I wrote with writers who create an outline and successively elaborate on that outline. Every time I had a new idea, the other writer said, "That's not in the outline."

I'm pretty sure that the third time I said, "I know, that's the point," the other writer was about ready to kill me. I was almost ready to commit murder myself. We agreed never to write together again.

Not every outliner does that. Some writers use an outline as a guide, and we can work together. I still get that itchy feeling, because I prefer not to use an outline.

7.6 Transform Your Perfection Rules

Throughout this book, I've suggested you aim to write well and publish. That means you avoid perfectionism. (Remember, Voltaire said, "Perfect is the enemy of the good.")

I learned to transform my perfection rules with the help of Weinberg's *Becoming a Technical Leader* WEI16.

Here is an example of a perfection rule for writing: I must always do a perfect job organizing my fieldstones.

Here's how to transform that rule:

1. State the rule precisely: "I *must* always do a perfect job organizing my fieldstones." That's a compulsion.
2. Instead of the compulsion, offer yourself a choice. Change the *must* to *can*. "I *can* always do a perfect job organizing my fieldstones."
3. Change the certainty in the "always" to possibility. "I can *sometimes* do a perfect job organizing my fieldstones."
4. Select three or more circumstances when you can follow this guide now:
   - If I know enough to do that part of the job.
   - If I can enlist others to help me do that job.
   - If the constraints around my work allow me to do the work.

Sometimes, I don't need to do anything except write the rule down. Then I look at it, laugh at myself, and boom, I transformed that rule. However, most writers don't have perfection rules about their fieldstones. More often, they have concerns that create fear, as back in Chapter 1.

Perfection rules prevent you from practicing your writing and publishing. If you worry that you are not perfect, remember that no writing can be perfect.

Now that you know about perfection rules, consider these writing traps.

7.7 Watch for These Writing Traps

Back in Chapter 1, I discussed some fears that writers might have and how writers might think they have "Writer's Block." Those fears and that idea of being blocked—those are writing traps.

As I work with writers, I also see these traps too often:

1. Waiting for the right idea.
2. Rewriting in the hope you can make it "perfect."
3. Editing before you finish writing.
4. Unfinished work.
5. Not publishing your writing.
6. Letting fear stop you from starting in the first place.

Here's how you can address these problems:

If you maintain an idea bank with fieldstones, you never have to wait for the "right" idea. You have tons of ideas. Pick one and write.

If you don't yet have any fieldstones, spend up to an hour listening to other people. I listen to podcasts, professional talks, and casual conversations. Sometimes, I ask people questions such as, "What do you wish you know about your job?" Write down at least one idea every five minutes.

What if you don't hear an idea every five minutes? Go meta, and write about why these conversations ramble and don't end.

You'll have plenty to write about.

The second trap is the rewriting trap to make your writing "perfect." Several times in this book, I've said that no piece of writing can be perfect. So reread the section before this. Write down your perfection rule and transform it. One way to stop seeking perfection is to choose three ideal readers and write one piece for each of them. Publish those pieces. Now, see what happens. I suspect your readers will be thrilled you wrote several perspectives about the same problem.

The third trap is about editing as you write. Instead, consider how to create and maintain your writing flow, your writer "trance." A writer trance helps you continue to write without editing. You might have heard the term "flow," from the book, *Flow: The Psychology of Optimal Experience* CSI08.

Here's how you might achieve flow and keep you in your writer trance:

- Shorten your writing timebox to five or six minutes and freewrite.
- At the end of the timebox, stand up and walk around for anywhere from 30 seconds to a minute.
- Then, return to your chair and write again in that same short timebox.

Continue the writing forward and walking. Don't cycle, because cycling might break your writer trance and allows you to edit. Instead, keep writing and walking until you finish as much as you can. Now, cycle through the piece, clarifying as you proceed. If you find yourself editing, stop and return to writing and walking.

The fourth trap is not finishing the writing all the way to publishing. When we don't finish a piece, we miss all the reinforcing of finishing small work to help us start and finish more. Amabile and Kramer discussed this in *The Progress Principle: Using Small Wins to Ignite Joy, Engagement, and Creativity at Work* AMA11. The more we make progress, the more we want to finish. In contrast, the less we make progress, the more the work hangs on. Remember, the longer the work takes, the longer it takes. (See the discussion in Chapter 2.)

You can avoid that by finishing and publishing. Back in Chapter 6, I suggested you have many places to use to publish your work. The act of publishing will help you avoid the rest of these traps. Publishing helps you realize nothing can ever be perfect—but your writing can help other people.

No product—and writing creates a product—is ever perfect. Don't let perfection be the enemy of the good. Do the best you can and publish it.

Besides, no one will put you in jail, even if you make a mistake.

7.8 Last Words—For Now

When I freed my inner writer, I gained many professional and personal benefits.

Professionally, my ideal readers have found my blogs and articles. Since I'm a consultant, they hired me to consult, coach, and speak. That was the point of starting to write, but it works.

In addition, I've learned what I think, in advance of any presentation I might give. I didn't babble my way through questions I had not yet considered. Now, I've often considered those questions.

Sometimes, those questions aren't part of *this* presentation. Other times, those questions relate, but are tangential, and I know how to introduce the tangent. My presentation skills improved as my writing improved. All because of the thinking and learning I did while writing.

In addition, I'm always surprised when clients explain how they found me. One client found me with just one article. I worked with them and the spinoffs from that company for over a decade.

I also gained personal benefits from freeing my inner writer. I learned how *I* create and reinforce my habits. I already knew how competitive I am with myself. Now I use that competitive streak in many areas of my life.

When you free your inner writer, you'll gain benefits you might not have considered.

Free your inner writer to educate, influence, and entertain your readers. Enjoy!

Annotated Bibliography

[AMA11] Amabile, Teresa and Steven Kramer. *The Progress Principle: Using Small Wins to Ignite Joy, Engagement, and Creativity at Work.* Harvard Business Review Press, Boston, 2011. They have completed the research that says we like to finish work in small chunks so we can make progress.

[CSI08] Csikszentmihalyi, Mihaly. *Flow: The Psychology of Optimal Experience.* HarperCollins Publishers, 2008. That magical state of flow, where you can finish work, separately or with others.

[COW16] Cowan, Nelson. *George Miller's Magical Number of Immediate Memory in Retrospect: Observations on the Faltering Progression of Science* in *Psychol Rev.* 2015 Jul; 122(3): 536–541. Retrieved online at https://www.ncbi.nlm.nih.gov/pmc/articles/PMC4486516/.

[FIS17] Fishman, Stephen. *The Copyright Handbook: What Every Writer Needs to Know.* Nolo Press. 2017. Fishman updates this book regularly. This is the version I own and refer to on a regular basis. Buy one. Read it. Search inside for various scenarios. Learn to protect your IP and exploit it.

[LAM07] Lamott, Anne. *Bird by Bird: Some Instructions On Writing and Life.* Anchor. 2007. Many other writers find her advice useful. I don't. As with most writing advice, your mileage will vary.

[MIL56] Miller, G. A. (1956). The magical number seven, plus or minus two: Some limits on our capacity for processing information. In *Psychological review*, 63(2), 81.

[NOT10] Noteberg, Staffan. *Pomodoro Technique Illustrated: The Easy Way to Do More in Less Time.* Pragmatic Bookshelf. 2010.

Wonderful introduction to a technique that helps you manage your work and finish it. Often, in less time than you imagined.

[MIH85] Miller, Robert B. and Stephen Heiman. *Strategic Selling: The Unique Sales System Proven Successful by America's Best Companies.* William Morrow, 1985. I first learned about the various buyers in 1988 and it totally changed how I thought of allies and people I perceived as obstacles. While you might not want to "sell" with your writing, this book might change how you think of people who are your ideal readers.

[MIN87] Minto, Barbara. *The Minto Pyramid Principle: Logic in Writing and Thinking.* Minto International, London. 1987. When I was learning to write, I found this structure useful to help me separate all my ideas into various articles.

[WEI16] Weinberg, Gerald M. *Becoming a Technical Leader.* I read the original book back in the 1990s, and I learned just from reading it. Now, as I've practiced many of the ideas, I'm a better human and a better leader. The rule transformation practice is just one of the many gems in this book.

[WCO14] Weinberg, Gerald M. *The Secrets of Consulting: A Guide to Giving and Getting Advice Successfully.* 2014. An excellent book for understanding what consulting is—and is not. And full of wonderful quotes about people, some of whom are your ideal readers.

[WCM14] Weinberg, Gerald M. *More Secrets of Consulting: The Consultant's Toolkit.* 2014. All about self-esteem. Writers need self-esteem to write and publish.

[WOW14] Weinberg, Gerald M. *Weinberg on Writing: The Fieldstone Method.* 2014. The first book I read about writing that made sense to me. When you write about something that matters to you, and you never start from a blank page, you can write anytime and anywhere.

More from Johanna

People know me as the "Pragmatic Manager." I help leaders and teams see simple and reasonable alternatives that might work in their context—often with a bit of humor. Equipped with that knowledge, they can decide how to adapt how they work.

See www.jrothman.com for my blogs and other writing.

If you liked this book, you might also like the other nonfiction books I've written:

Management Books:

- *Practical Ways to Manage Yourself: Modern Management Made Easy, Book 1*
- *Practical Ways to Lead and Serve—Manage—Others: Modern Management Made Easy, Book 2*
- *Practical Ways to Lead an Innovative Organization: Modern Management Made Easy, Book 3*
- *Behind Closed Doors: Secrets of Great Management*
- *Hiring Geeks That Fit*

Product Development:

- *From Chaos to Successful Distributed Agile Teams: Collaborate to Deliver*
- *Create Your Successful Agile Project: Collaborate, Measure, Estimate, Deliver*
- *Manage Your Project Portfolio: Increase Your Capacity and Finish More Projects, 2nd ed*
- *Agile and Lean Program Management: Scaling Collaboration Across the Organization*

- *Diving for Hidden Treasures: Uncovering the Cost of Delay Your Project Portfolio*
- *Predicting the Unpredictable: Pragmatic Approaches to Estimating Project Cost or Schedule*
- *Project Portfolio Tips: Twelve Ideas for Focusing on the Work You Need to Start & Finish*
- *Manage It!: Your Guide to Modern, Pragmatic Project Management*

Personal Development:

- *Free Your Inner Nonfiction Writer*
- *Become a Successful Independent Consultant*
- *Write a Conference Proposal*
- *Manage Your Job Search*

I'd like to stay in touch with you. If you don't already subscribe, please sign up for my email newsletter, the Pragmatic Manager. Please connect with me on LinkedIn, or follow me on Twitter, @johannarothman.

If you're interested in the writing workshop that goes with this book, see Free Your Inner Writer.

Did this book help you? If so, please consider writing a review of it. Reviews help other readers find books. Thanks!

Johanna

www.ingramcontent.com/pod-product-compliance
Lightning Source LLC
Chambersburg PA
CBHW072039110526
44592CB00012B/1487